D0865569

LESSONS OF A TOP PRODUCER

Don Watson

Copyright © 2014 by Don Watson.

All rights reserved. No part of this book may be reproduced, scanned, or distributed in any printed or electronic form without permission.

First Edition: June 2014

Suncoast Digital Press, Inc.
Sarasota, FL

Printed in the United States of America

ISBN: 978-1-939237-28-6

ABOUT THE AUTHOR

Don Watson has been in the financial services industry since 1988, when he began his career as an intern at a regional investment bank in Cincinnati, Ohio. After six years at the wire houses, he entered the bank brokerage arena just as they were entering into the brokerage business. There were a lot of growing pains, as traditional bankers didn't know how to handle this new crop of young, aggressive sales professionals who ran with their own maverick ideas rather than following the norm.

With original compensation structures still in place, Watson and some of his fellow Financial Advisors quickly became the highest paid individuals in the bank, causing some tension between more traditional lines of business. Here he learned valuable lessons in relationship management, diplomacy, and leadership.

After seven years of working as a bank Financial Advisor, he was offered the Regional Director position for an entirely new region obtained through an acquisition. Watson built that program from the ground up, overseeing licensing and registrations, compliance, staffing, and eventually sales. As often happens in this industry, that bank was sold to an institution that did not yet offer investment services—Watson presumed this was a fortuitous opportunity.

Unfortunately, they had no desire to offer these services, as they were a very traditional, foreign-owned institution, so his career took him to another regional bank, once again, as a Financial Advisor. In this incredibly well-organized firm Watson learned the valuable lesson of how using an effective model to its fullest potential can produce excellent results by working smarter, not harder.

Another lesson—a hard lesson—was that the only constant is that things change, and he gained an even deeper appreciation of supportive, well-working environments when, one day, his company merged with their largest competitor and changed the entire program to an ineffective model.

Sometimes setbacks can cause great opportunities, which is what happened next. Watson spent the following two years helping community banks enter the investment world through the use of Third Party Providers, or TPPs. This represented a source of revenue that was unknown to the community banking world and one that had low capital requirements, minimal risk, and large upside potential. He eventually went on to run the wealth division of one of those institutions, where one of his responsibilities was to create and implement a business plan consisting of the entire wealth division, including private banking, investment management and brokerage. Lessons of a Top Producer is based on that proven business plan.

In addition to Watson's personal success, the feedback from those who Watson personally coached was so positive that he organized the practices and systems into one file and began writing his program. *Lessons of a Top Producer* is his first published book, and lays the groundwork for his comprehensive sales training program, the Apollo Sales Training, to be released in October, 2014. Whether leading a seminar at a trade event, giving a keynote speech, or coaching an individual, Watson is consistent with his message of personal connection, and has facts at hand to prove that his approach works.

Watson currently resides in Sarasota, Florida with his wife and children. He is an avid golfer and fisherman, Tampa Bay Rays fan, lives and dies by Cincinnati Bearcat basketball, loves the arts, and has been overheard to say he should've been a chef.

TABLE OF CONTENTS

FOREWORD

"Find out what works, and do it over and over until you're the best."

I picked up this gem of advice during my 25 years of working in the world of Top Producers, and those that aspire to become Top Producers, and it has served me well. This is what came to mind as I was reading the way Don Watson has distilled so many decades of tried-and-true *Lessons* into this "playbook."

In my career, I have accumulated over two decades of experience as a Financial Advisor working at the largest global investment banks, regional B/D's, and a private start-up advising institutional accounts with billions in assets; in the process, I have learned many of these lessons myself. I've experienced many different management styles, methods of obtaining new clients, and various systems used, misused, and ignored. Watson has a refreshing, simple approach I think will appeal to anyone success-minded enough to pick up this book.

I met Don Watson eight years ago. During this time a few things stuck out about his approach that stood out from the norm in financial sales business. He, like me, never seemed to be in the office. My old boss at PaineWebber said to me, "Put yourself in the place of most potential." That is Watson's approach as well. Whether he is at a Chamber of Commerce event or an Economic Development Council meeting, or wherever that "place of most potential" is, you will find Don. Sitting in your office waiting for someone to walk in, cold-calling or sending emails (contrary to some opinions) doesn't always produce the best results. As Watson describes wonderfully in this book, go find the money and get involved with that crowd. Dress for success and live the part. Find out what works and do it over and over until you're the best.

Watson doesn't mean to underplay the necessary knowledge of investment portfolio construction however. You've all heard the acronym K.I.S.S. (keep it simple, stupid). Clients want to know that you know, and if you're reading this book, you probably do. Clients don't want to know too. (When you go to the doctor's office for a checkup, you don't want to be the doctor—you want the doctor to be the doctor!) Watson keeps it simple, and after reading this highly intelligent book, you should be doing the same.

Lessons of a Top Producer is about building relationships, earning trust, and systematically capturing the clients you want to build the best practice in your area. If you read and apply these Lessons, you will be the "Financial Guy/ Girl" in your market.

—Geoffrey Shea
Former investment manager, 25 years

INTRODUCTION

Perhaps you've noticed, as I have during my 26-year career in financial services, that some things are totally out of your control. Bank mergers, market cycles, and economic conditions are just a few of the hurdles that financial advisors must jump on a constant basis. Program directors are saddled with high turnover, lower fees, and constantly changing compliance regulation.

The one thing that has remained relatively constant over the years is the sales process; it simply gets overlooked by many institutions. I've always found it amusing when a sales manager asks their advisors what they can do to increase revenue. The usual response is that they need to spend more time with clients and prospects, and less time dealing with "TPS reports" (to borrow a term from the movie *Office Space*). Contradictory to the need, the normal response from management is—more product training.

This book addresses the needs of the financial advisor from a pure sales perspective. It starts with support from the top of the management spectrum, and ends with the front line sales professional. As with any business model, implementation and accountability are the keys to success. This book will address not only the concepts, but the feedback that is instrumental in fine-tuning a program in order to build a truly successful operation.

As I said, industry sales processes have not evolved and are woefully inefficient even with our era's amazing advances in technology. Let's briefly review the relevant recent history of our industry: In 1993, banks began to form their own brokerage divisions, either in-house or through Third Party Providers (TPPs), which basically tested the Glass-Steagall Act of 1933. The act was presented by Senator Carter Glass, the former U.S. Treasury Secretary and founder of the Federal Reserve System. After an amendment permitting bank deposit insurance, the act gained the support of Chairman Henry Bascom Steagall of the House

Banking and Currency Committee. The act was originally passed to prevent banking institutions from engaging in "commercial speculation."

Banks would continuously loan funds to companies in which they had invested, causing a large amount of risk exposure to the bank depositors. Like many government regulations, the act had major side effects. In fact, shortly after it was passed, Glass himself reportedly moved to repeal the act, claiming it was an "overreaction" and far too harsh.

In the early 1990s, banks began to test the act by providing brokerage services to their clients either through their own broker dealers or TPPs. By 1999, the Glass-Steagall Act was repealed and replaced with the Gramm-Leach-Baily Act, which, among other things, allowed banks to offer investment services. By then, virtually every commercial bank was already offering them, and within a few short years, it became a very lucrative line of business for many financial institutions. Many of them had well-established trust departments that had been in place for many years; however, the brokerage business was something entirely new to most organizations.

Over the last 20 years, banks have implemented many different platforms to provide investment services. However, most of them have underperformed their wire house counterparts. With all of the advantages banking programs have to offer, they should be exceeding the regional wire houses in revenue production. However, on average, they underachieve.

The financial services industry has changed dramatically in the past 25 years, moving from something that only a small portion of the population needed, to something that encompasses nearly everyone in the working class. I can recall being a young intern at a small regional investment bank, when Fridays were a key day in the markets. The only reason for this was that a positive close meant a good weekend for clients, as the only time they checked the prices on their investments was on Sunday (it was printed in the newspaper). Today, prices are readily available to anyone who wants a quote with just the click of a button or a quick peek at a smartphone. Back then, financial news was only available at the end of the traditional news cycle and was covered in less than five minutes. Today, there are dozens of 24-hour networks providing news and advice on virtually any type of investment.

So if someone today can order lunch and then buy 100 shares of Apple while their club sandwich is being prepared, why do we need financial advisors? The cost of the transaction was probably less than their lunch tab, and it was executed in real time without calling a broker, financial advisor, or any middleman.

The term "broker" is defined as:

An agent who buys or sells for a principal on a commission basis, without having title to the property.

The definition was much more accurate in the early days, as we basically executed trades for clients. Yes, we recommended purchases and sales, and had analysts and traders telling us when to buy and sell, but the compensation was based on the actual transaction, not the advice. Today, anyone can execute the transaction; however, not everyone has the valuable advice.

The intent of this book is to provide a "playbook" for financial professionals from a pure sales perspective. Rather than more information, this is about a strategy and how to apply it. This book is not about compliance or operations, with the exception of how these impact the sales process. *Lessons of a Top Producer* provides a distilled, systematic approach to the sales process, which starts with upper management and filters through all of the sales professionals within your organization.

Over the years, I have read countless books about financial sales, many of which are very thorough and well-written. However, there is one glaring gap in nearly all of them—the action plan is limited, and there's no emphasis on accountability. In the playbook analogy, this would be like giving a wide receiver the general idea they should run down the field and if a football drops into their hands, they should try not to drop it, but if they do—there is no real consequence. This is the "method" and attitude I have seen over and over, and you probably know exactly what I'm talking about.

Just because I write down on a piece of paper that I want to have ten new introductions next week doesn't mean it will actually happen. One must set objectives that are specific, and have an action plan for achieving them. Accountability, by the way, is not about fault, praise, blame, shame or guilt. Rather, one can choose to be held accountable for achieving results that indicate you are achieving success, as you've defined it. In that way, accountability is a powerful and effective tool, creating the condition that supports your commitment rather than your moods. This book will show you how to do just that.

This book is not about being a financial advisor, private banker, insurance agent, or good old stockbroker. My valuable advice is not how to do your job; it's about how to do your job efficiently and effectively to be more successful. It's about a systematic approach to a sales process designed to get YOU where YOU want to be. The goals and objectives of an individual are exactly that—individual. Some may want more money to support their families or to take more world-class vacations, and there's nothing wrong with that ambition. Some may be after power and respect, while other competitive individuals just want to be "The Best" at what they do.

As a sales manager in the Southeastern U.S., I encountered so many different individual objectives that I could write a whole other book just based on the goals of my employees. In a rural town in Alabama, I had an advisor that consistently produced about $200,000 per year in gross production, well under our minimum guidelines. After countless hours of coaching and sales training, I realized that there was a production plateau which was almost certainly not going to be improved upon.

Rather than only looking at his numbers, I looked at the man and discovered that he was one of the most prominent figures in his community. His $60,000 per year income made him one the most highly compensated people in town, and he was quite philanthropic with his funds. He was a deacon at the local church, and well known and respected by everyone in the community. Without doing a great deal of research, I realized that he was "the financial guy" in that market. What I didn't realize early on was that he had achieved his own objectives at a level that may make most advisors pursue other interests. I'm not implying that lower levels of production are acceptable in all instances, only that objectives in business and in life are truly individual by nature.

The goal of this book is to provide a systematic approach to life and business. We will begin by addressing the vision of the individual. The concept of "what do you want to be when you grow up" will be taken to levels with a realistic approach of how to achieve your goals. We will also venture into the "firm" and the way financial services organizations are organized and managed. For all of you sales managers out there who are trying to squeeze every dollar of revenue out of your sales force, how do you motivate them to succeed? Are your methods helping the process or harming it?

The first chapter of this book begins with defining your business purpose. The more clarity you have, the faster your success track.

In the second chapter, we will look at compensation structures. As sales professionals, we need to have a clear understanding of exactly how we will earn money, and when we will get paid that money, and often this is not the case. Management could be the problem, or the solution, and we'll look at the manager's role as "coach."

The next two chapters are *Lessons* especially for the individual advisor about how to get in the way of opportunities by positioning yourself to attract your desired clientele.

We will then venture down the path of the sales cycle, from the time an introduction is made to the ongoing maintenance of a client relationship, and how to tap your best possible referral sources.

The next two chapters address the issue that hinders everyone's ability to succeed: time. No matter how successful you are, where you attended college, or how much money you have in the bank, time is equally distributed among everyone. It's what you do with those 24 hours that makes the difference. We will go into detail about using that customer relationship management (CRM) system that you probably have access to, but just never use. (Every bank that I have been associated with in the past ten years has had a CRM system, some proprietary, and others generic, and none have ever used it—not one in ten years.)

Finally, before we put it all together and form an action plan for tomorrow, we'll peek into your own house and make sure certain things are in order. We'll take goal-setting to a whole new level, one of reason and accountability. By following my advice, when you write down your tasks for the week, they won't just be arbitrary, but attainable, and they'll each have a set plan for success.

The final chapter takes you into my world and explains the importance of ongoing training and accountability—not from your employer, but rather your coach and advocate, someone who has no political agenda and just one ambition: to help you get to where you want to be.

For over 25 years I have helped clients achieve their financial ambitions through financial and investment planning. The next 25 will be spent helping advisors achieve their ambitions through coaching, training, and ongoing accountability for activities. If you're ready to take your practice to the next level, study this playbook and live your life to its fullest potential.

Chapter 1
DEFINE YOUR BUSINESS PURPOSE

If you've been in the financial services industry for any period of time, you've probably had a sales manager ask you to define "what you do." Maybe they called it a "personal brand" or an "elevator speech." Regardless of what it was called, they probably never told you how to develop it, phrase it, or even think of it, for that matter. The premise, however, is still vital, as it is not intended to be simply a one-liner that will bring in clients; it is something to help you define the type of clients that you intend to pursue.

Financial institutions attract a wide variety of consumers, from the extremely wealthy to those living paycheck-to-paycheck, all of whom are in the arena we call "customers." It's a relatively odd marketing structure when you think about it. If we look at nearly all other consumer organizations, most have a specific demographic as their clientele.

There's a skate shop just across the street from my office that I can be fairly certain doesn't do a lot of direct marketing to the retirement home just a few blocks away. From restaurants to car dealerships to retail clothing shops, most businesses have a specific and identifiable demographic for their products or services. Their marketing resources and efforts can be honed to effectively reach that target market. Financial institutions, specifically banks, don't have that luxury. National and regional commercial banks have clientele from all walks of life, all with different economic standing and very different needs. Community and "niche" style banks are somewhat unique, but for the most part, most consumers have a checking account someplace.

As financial advisors, our business purpose may be defined in part by the organization that we work for, and also by our own definition of personal success. If these are not in harmony with one another, this can cause tension and frustration for both employer and employee. About 10 years ago, banks

1

decided to go shopping for broker dealers in order to increase noninterest income for the institution. The idea was to take top-performing financial advisors and place them in an environment with a vibrant referral stream coming from other lines of business. The results were mixed at best, and at worst, a disaster. It wasn't due to culture shock or a different management style; it was due to conflicting visions between the institution and the advisor.

The bank operated like, well—a bank. Take a successful wire house advisor, assign them five branches over 100 miles of territory, and tell them they need to do teller training instead of attending the monthly Chamber of Commerce meetings…see what happens. Better yet, tell him he can no longer play in his Wednesday morning golf league at his country club due to the mandatory weekly conference call for branch managers. This is a formula for failure, and it's mostly due to the conflict in different visions of success.

When I was first offered a financial advisor position in Sarasota, Florida, I had visions of being on a yacht fishing for tuna in the Gulf of Mexico while asking a wealthy prospect "what do I need to do in order to earn a piece of your business?" That was defining my business purpose. I had the same vision of that conversation occurring at a country club while getting ready to tee off on the first hole. What do these two visions have in common? They both involve opportunities for one-on-one conversations with high-net-worth people in a social setting. That bears repeating: My vision of success in my business was of me having one-on-one conversations with wealthy people in social settings.

Neither vision involved sitting in a bank branch selling fixed annuities to CD customers. So, if the bank you work for isn't equipped to give you the vision for your own business success, it must be up to you. Not even another advisor can do it for you.

In Northern Alabama, I had a well-seasoned advisor that went through the exercise of articulating his vision, and the outcome was quite different than my own. His ideal situation or vision was having his calendar completely booked with new prospective clients at every branch that he was assigned, and having a full time assistant process everything that was sold. His vision had nothing to do with social interactions and was very transactional by nature. His clientele were not necessarily wealthy types; in fact, the opposite was more likely. His demographic of clientele were limited in assets and financial acumen, which is exactly who he felt comfortable dealing with. So, I ask, would joining the local country club get this advisor any closer to his vision, or would it actually deter him from it?

This is an example of how defining your business purpose helps you to form an activity plan that is right for you. Similar to a workout routine, if your vision is to wind up with amazing six-pack abs, your activities (exercises) must be customized to that purpose. With a different vision in mind, the routine would be different. As I mentioned earlier, in 2001 I was transferred to Sarasota, Florida, in order to form the brokerage platform for a regional bank. After about six months of getting to know all of the local players, I was invited by a commercial lender to an offshore loan closing. At the time, I wasn't aware that if certain loans were closed offshore(meaning out of the state of Florida) specific taxes could be avoided. With ease of access to charter boats and year-round mostly great weather, this was somewhat common practice at the time. The day of the charter, I found myself sitting on a yacht, fishing for tuna, asking a high-net-worth prospect what I could do to earn a piece of his business. My vision had become reality!

I wasn't even sure how I got there. However, I knew how I could get back there again. After that successful voyage, I offered to pay for all offshore closings for all the lenders at the bank and averaged about two per month from that day forward. Thirteen years later, I have noticed that the bulk of my clients have a few things in common. They all love to fish and golf, and the vast majority of client meetings take place outside of the office. Notice this is the opposite of what my Northern Alabama advisor preferred, yet each (and any) vision can lead to great success if the corresponding activities are consistently done.

Another reason to define our business purpose is to insure that our efforts and resources match the currently required role within an organization. If your vision is similar to mine and your current role requires you to cover numerous branch locations, train branch staff, and cover a large number of clients, you may have an inherent contradiction. I can say with some certainty that you will not achieve your vision, as it is not in harmony with your current role. Such a conflict can be resolved by changing your vision, or by finding a new position with responsibilities aligned with your vision.

Only you can define the business purpose which, when envisioned, feels right for you. It can motivate you very differently than if an institution or someone else defines it for you—it is a carrot, not a stick.

As you do this exercise, I recommend that you ask yourself questions that don't just relate to money. Money, for most people, is a means to an end. You want it for some reason other than just to have it, and in most cases, it's not even about the material items that you purchase. This is not always the case, but I find with major purchases, there's an underlying reason for the desire to obtain virtually any item. So I would ask you not to pin up a photo of a luxury car on your wall and say, "that's what I'm after." Instead, focus on the lifestyle that you would like to have for you and your family. Does it involve a moderately priced home in the suburbs, or a beachfront condo? Again, don't think of it as material items; think of it as a way of life.

When you write down your vision of your own personal utopia, don't edit—you just need to build the roads to get there. The Lessons in this book will show you exactly how to build those roads and navigate them successfully to your personal success.

Your activity plan is based on your vision for your business.

Chapter 2
MANAGER AS COACH

As with any business, success usually begins with management and works its way down. We won't spend a great deal of time on leadership as it has so much content that it could be the topic of another book. However, it is important to look at how leadership interactions and business models affect the sales force and their ultimate success.

When dealing with financial advisors, you must consider what they encounter on a regular day. Some have a very sporadic income and this can be very stressful, regardless of the paycheck's size. Most compensation models are commission-based, and the advisor is usually paid monthly. (One annuity chargeback in a month can be the difference between getting a paycheck or not.) Most employees, especially in a bank environment, don't have to deal with this issue. Commercial lenders, private bankers, business bankers, and retail staff are normally compensated via a salary, plus a possible quarterly or annual bonus. On a side note, I have noticed recently that several banks have converted the advisors' compensation structure to their more traditional salary-plus-bonus system. Time will tell whether this new strategy will be successful.

Advisors have two unique forms of compensation. The first is transaction-based fees, and is based on the sale of specific products. The purchase of individual securities, such as stocks, bonds, options, mutual funds, unit trusts and annuities, fits into this spectrum. Other unique products, such as certain hedge funds and hedging contracts, also fit into this category. Some of these products have created hybrid versions to fit into the new fee-based model that is becoming so prevalent to financial organizations. Nearly all mutual funds have a "C share" model that is designed to pay larger trailer compensation than up-front fees. A few variable annuities now offer a fee-based model with no surrender charges and large ongoing fees. However, most are stripped of their most compelling attributes, such as lifetime income guarantees and special death benefits.

The second form of compensation is the ongoing fee-based structure. This seems to be the wave of the future for financial organizations as this form of income is more beneficial for the institution. Bank trust departments have been in this business for years; however, they are limited in their capabilities, as many products simply are not available within this type of platform. From a brokerage perspective, these products are generally sold through a Registered Investment Advisor (RIA) platform. Most have an open architecture component, meaning you can purchase just about anything in the accounts as long as they are in harmony with the overall portfolio structure. These accounts have become commonplace in the investment world as there are no front-end fees, somewhat minimal withdrawal fees, and a wide variety of products. As for the compensation structure, advisors usually get an advance on first-year fees, plus an ongoing fee after year one. However, this is not always the case, as some institutions will compensate on actual dollar revenue crediting, meaning when the client pays the fee, the advisor gets credit to the commission grid.

The reason I point out compensation structures is because I am constantly amazed at the number of department heads that have no idea how this works. I am not recommending one type of compensation over another, as they each have benefits and pitfalls. The individual stock picking business has gone the way of the dodo bird, as financial advisors have a difficult time being competitive on pricing, and the sheer volume of work needed to be successful is exorbitant. We continue to find mutual fund buyers out there, and variable annuity volume has continued to increase even in this time of closer scrutiny. The interesting point about variable annuities is that they actually do provide a service for their higher fees. It's a matter of great debate as to whether the attributes are worth the cost. However, whatever side of the debate you're on, annuities do offer unique benefits not available in any other product.

Plenty of financial institutions have had nothing but praise for the merits of fee-based advising—albeit with ulterior motives. Just to clarify, I am a vibrant supporter of RIA products; however, I don't feel they should be the only option of any institution. Whether an institution is a public or privately-held company, they all are aware of their respective stock valuation. For a public company, the reasons are obvious, but the privately-held community bank also has an incentive, perhaps more so than their public counterparts. Currently, investment banks value fee-based revenue from their respective wealth units at about 14 times earnings. Transactional- based revenue is valued at about eight. This means, in dollar terms, that if your department makes $1 million in profit (and it's all fee-based), you'd have $14 million in equity value for the institution, whereas the transactional based business would have a mere $8 million in value.

It's likely that your own program is a hybrid of both types of revenue, but you can see why your CEO focus may be leaning more towards fee-based revenue than transactional. Just because your company isn't publicly traded, don't feel as though you're exempt from this valuation. Community bankers get hounded by investment bankers wanting to either take them public or sell them, and this valuation is like gold to their shareholders. To put this into perspective, take a look at the chart below and the stockholder value added through fee based asset management accounts.

Yearly Gross Revenues		$5,000,000		
Product	Product Mix %	Gross Revenue	Margin (25%)	Stockholder Value
Variable Annuity	30%	$ 1500,000	$ 375,000	$ 3,000,000
Fixed Annuity	20%	$ 1,000,000	$ 250,000	$ 2,000,000
Mutual Fund	10%	$ 500,000	$ 125,000	$ 1,000,000
Individual Security	10%	$ 500,000	$ 125,000	$ 1,000,000
Asset Management	**30%**	**$ 1,500,000**	**$ 375,000**	**$ 5,250,000**

This chart is based on $5 million in gross dealer concession (GDC) derived from different product categories; whereas asset management fees incur a multiple of 14 and all else only eight. Another consideration is the distribution cost of each product. The data is calculated based on a 25% profit margin which includes a financial advisor payout on a standard grid.

In reality, the distribution cost of asset management accounts are substantially lower, as many trust officer positions are salaried and have a significantly lower cost than the traditional financial advisor. Although this is a broad stroke example, you can see why certain investment accounts are vitally important to your CEO, regardless of whether your institution is a public company or a community bank with limited shareholders. Increases in share value opens doors to CEOs for additional capital, acquisitions, and compensation increases, which contributes to the support of certain types of investment products. The table shows average production at a community bank with corresponding product mix. Note the increase in shareholder value provided through the asset management program, regardless of whether it's generated through an RIA or internal trust department.

Now that you know about certain revenue sources and how they impact shareholder value, let's venture into the management of your sales force.

Financial advisors, private bankers, trust BDOs, and many other financial professions are extremely isolated in their endeavors. In many instances, there are few support systems they can rely on for consultation and support. This is more prevalent in the banking world than in their wire house counterparts, which generally work in a single location, allowing for personal interaction with peers in the same profession.

This is something to consider when recruiting advisors within a bank platform. Bank program directors are notorious for hiring top-producing wire house brokers that often fail to deliver within the banking world. You would think it would be a perfect match; however, the isolation and lack of communication among a similar peer group prove to be the downfall of the relationship.

As managers, we must make certain that a support system is in place for direct interaction with your advisors. Nearly all programs have some sort of weekly sales call with their subordinates as a group. However, individual interaction is often overlooked, and sometimes has negative connotations associated with the interactions. I have spoken with many bank employees that have shared with me their only direct interaction with their supervisor is associated with negative issues. This is not motivation—it's intimidation, whether it's intentional or not.

I realize that geographical, economic and time restraints hinder the in-person meeting structure, but it is an invaluable activity that should not be sidelined. In our modern world of electronic communication, we find ourselves interacting with people that we've never seen, or even spoken with, on a regular basis. This system is perfectly adequate when dealing with operational tasks that don't require personal relationships.

However, when dealing with salespeople, some method of one-to-one communication is not something one can replace with a group conference call. It's an opportunity to build rapport, mutual respect, and be an advocate to your staff which means less roadblocks to high productivity.

About 20 years ago, while employed as a financial advisor in the Midwest, I found myself working diligently on two large cases that were taking a great deal of time. Considering the size of the cases, it was justified, until I had no revenue posting over halfway through the month. Finally, at the end of the month, one of the cases transferred in and was about to credit my grid just as the client changed their mind. We had had some operational issues regarding the transfer, which ultimately led to the undoing of the company-client relationship.

A few days before the end of the month, my sales manager showed up at my primary branch and asked if we could speak for a moment. I honestly thought I was going to get fired on the spot. I had very little in revenue for the month, and hadn't spoken to my manager in quite some time. He asked me about my revenue numbers for the month and inquired as to the reason for the dismal performance. I explained the issues around the cases and the great deal of time I had devoted to each, only to lose one in the final hour. His response was a simple one: "What can I do to help?"

I've had over 25 years of financial service, but I remember that conversation like it was yesterday. My sales manager wasn't acting like a supervisor. He was acting like a coach—someone who was there not to criticize my actions, but to help me move forward. Instead of kicking me when I was down, he put out his hand and sure enough, I jumped right back into the game with renewed determination.

Sometimes I wonder if the term "sales manager" is an oxymoron. When I served in that role, my primary responsibility was to manage the staff of financial sales representatives, including financial advisors, private bankers and trust BDOs. Sounds simple enough, but in reality I interviewed candidates, estimated budget numbers, signed expense reports, and met with other department heads either in person or via conference calls. I managed people, not sales. Even more to the point, I managed conversations, especially conversations the sales people were having with themselves about their sales-generating activity plans, incentives, and motivating goals.

This book is about being an advocate to your team and helping them achieve their goals, acting more like a "sales coach" than a sales manager.

11

Coaches help people aspire to levels they never thought possible. Would an Olympic athlete ever consider *not* having a coach? Of course not. Coaches actually work for you, not the other way around. A coach is not there to micromanage activities or dictate personal goals—a coach uses a unique set of skills to help the person they are coaching achieve their personal best. That's the premise of this book, and it all starts at the top.

So, in your role as a sales coach, what steps do you take on a consistent basis to help your sales force succeed? As with most important undertakings, it is a good idea to first take stock of what is true, now. What is the "mood" of your staff? Certain circumstances are difficult to manage, and perhaps your organization has internal issues that impact the mood. I will warn you about the pitfalls of trying to change an organization because I have fallen into that pit a few times myself.

Seemingly simple tasks can sometimes be so cumbersome that you can't believe how long it's been done that way. Recently, I was involved with an organization that took two weeks to do anything. Open a new brokerage or asset management account? Two weeks. Just a simple fund disbursement? Two weeks. The processes were so cumbersome and completely outdated that I wrote a report on how to fix the problems virtually instantaneously. This company had been operating with this inefficient model for seven years. The only way to change any problem is to first admit there is one, and nobody likes to be told they're doing something wrong. My report didn't get very far up the food chain because there were a lot of people in the way that would need to say "yes, this is better," and that rarely happens in large organizations. Welcome to the politics of big banking.

So now that you know the pitfalls, what can you do that is *within your control* that will help your staff reach the desired levels of achievement? A great place to start is to coach them to define their business purpose, as discussed in the previous chapter, and to find their niche in the marketplace, which is covered in the next chapter. Once you ask your advisors about the type of clientele they want to obtain and how they intend to pursue them, you will know what coaching and advice to provide.

One piece of advice applicable to all your advisors is to encourage their community involvement, based on their desired interests. If they're seeking business owners, the local chamber of commerce or economic development council (EDC) can be great organizations and generally easy to get involved in. If retirees are their niche, the arts, such as the symphony or ballet, may be a good place to start. Many of these organizations are minimal cost and can produce astounding dividends. Beyond the level of consistent participation, you can coach the advisor to take leadership (more high-profile) roles and even become a board member. You can help pave the way into these organizations with a simple letter of recommendation to the board chairs.

Over the years I have served on countless nonprofit boards and other civic organizations within my community, some of them for business development purposes, others for philanthropic reasons, and many just because I wanted to. Unless you write a big check to an organization, you generally have to be appointed to a board through either an invitation or application. The invitation side is easy—someone thinks that your serving on the board would be beneficial for their organization, possibly for your unique knowledge of a certain topic that would be practical for the organization, or maybe your community contacts of possible donors. If you are applying for a board position, it can be similar to applying for a job. Your competition consists of the local city councilman and the grandson of the family that just donated a building. Your advisors may not get on every board they want, but you can help them try.

Coach your staff to track both the activities and the results being achieved through their community involvement and have that reported to you. It's irrelevant how wonderful or exclusive an organization is; involvement is the key. I have spoken to so many institutions that simply stopped supporting civic organizations because they didn't feel it was being quantified. They had no method of tracking successes and failures, and no concept of which individuals from their organization were even involved. As leaders or coaches we must support our staff in their civic endeavors, track activities, and, most importantly, quantify results. This will also help to motivate your staff as well, and when results begin to present themselves you may find them taking on more and more civic responsibility. As a side benefit, this generally will also provide some free positive press for your advisors and your company. In later chapters you will learn how to build your Customer Relationship Management (CRM) systems to track both activities and results with accurate, relevant data.

Now that you know how to be an advocate and coach to your advisors, what about the not-so-comfortable assignment of dealing with underperformance? This is the duty of the sales manager that is generally not the highlight of your day. There is no one-size-fits-all method as each situation is unique. For example, I have managed sales staff in both wire houses and bank programs and they are like night and day.

Generally speaking, a lack of performance in a wire house leads to an attrition separation, meaning the advisor runs out of money and moves on. This can take a little more time in a bank environment, as most advisors are on some type of salary plus commission. Poor performance in a bank environment can be caused by many factors, such as poor leadership in the branch or region, low branch traffic (which is often the case with newer branches), and poor financial advisor ability. In order to solve the problems of an underperforming region, you must first ascertain the cause of the underperformance. Banks are notorious for continually replacing staff with no regard as to the cause.

While doing a research project for a large northeastern financial institution, it was apparent that in one specific region their performance was dismal, and they were running an astonishing 300% turnover rate in just two years. A turnover rate like that indicates a problem with structure, and unless you're the worst recruiter in the world, it probably has very little to do with your hires.

When banks come into new markets they do it one of two ways, either through acquisition or building branches which are de novo (Latin for "new," used in banking). When analyzing branch circuits, I always ask whether the branches are seasoned branches (that is, over five years old), or de novo branches, which helps to ascertain the performance reality of each branch. Seasoned branches, depending on how long the branch has been there, will already have clients, whereas a de novo branch would have none, and thus presents unique challenges.

In the case of the aforementioned northeastern organization, the branch circuit was acquired with a unique caveat—they had no investment services at all. The bank leadership thought this to be a golden opportunity for the introduction of the wealth management division and structured their marketing plan accordingly. They actively trained staff to identify qualified referrals to send to their advisors, and compensated them accordingly. It seemed as though they were doing the right things, but they were having horrid results. It took some very focused study to realize some of the problems that existed within the entire platform.

The average advisor in the region covered a 200 square mile territory, and through company mandate, each branch was visited weekly. Advisors were averaging 1,000 miles per week and were not reimbursed for mileage (frankly, I'm not necessarily sure if that's even legal, but we won't get into that). This was also a commission-based platform that paid a small draw every two weeks, and according to my calculations, it covered the fuel cost for the circuit. Forgetting the monetary aspect for a moment, consider the windshield time. At 50 mph, that's 20 hours a week in a car. Typically, most of that driving time is done either during early morning hours or after the branches close. It may have been a welcome break, considering that they had nearly six hours in conference calls scheduled each week which were generally scheduled during the early morning hours. These calls consisted of a financial advisor call, private banking call, product call, regional retail banking call, and branch manager call (your circuit). Nearly all of these calls were redundant, as many featured the same participants. This is a great example of senior leadership instructing subordinates to "communicate" with their staff, and this was the "solution."

In a conversation with a senior manager of the retail program, I was astonished to discover that one day every week he had nothing but conference calls on his calendar. They were each one hour long, and there were six scheduled every Tuesday. In later chapters we're going to cover some lessons and tips in time management, and I can promise they won't consist of long drives and conference calls, but rather prospecting and client interactions.

The secondary reason for the region's lack of performance was due to inadequate direct leadership. You would think that with all of the conference calls there would be interactions between the sales managers and their advisors—that was not the case at all. In fact, many advisors reported that other than the group conference calls, there were few or no interactions with the sales manager assigned to the region. The same was true with the retail branch managers, as they also reported little if any contact with the regional sales manager. I would assume he spent a great deal of time interviewing candidates. We have a tendency to preach to our advisors that they must be seen to be known and this is also the case with sales managers. If you have a struggling advisor and they feel that no one is there to assist, they're sure to be looking for another job soon.

In the case of this institution, they just continued to recruit new advisors to replace the ones that left, without ever addressing the issues at hand. Did they assume this high turnover was normal and acceptable? Some of the issues in this example could be dealt with at local levels. Other issues, such as mileage reimbursement and coverage areas, may need to be addressed at higher levels. A few years ago, LPL Financial reported that branch efficiencies peaked at three branches per financial advisor. Now, this can be a self-fulfilling prophecy in which successful advisors will voluntarily cut branch circuits as their production increases, allowing them to focus attention on a larger client base and more successful branches. *Post hoc ergo propter hoc*—one event doesn't always cause the other.

Look at the chain of events that occurred in this institution. After the acquisition, 13 financial advisors, two private bankers, and one trust officer were hired to cover the new territory. Two years later, all of the advisors, one private banker, and one trust officer had vacated their positions. That is just shy of a 100% turnover rate for the original hires in just 24 months. The turnover rate is actually higher due to the fact that the financial advisors were replaced, and new hires subsequently resigned within the same time period. Turnover can be a cancer to an organization, even if it's apparently isolated to a single area.

These events generate high internal costs, as each new hire must be trained, and everyone experiences a period of transitional time in which revenue production is a secondary concern. It also causes time inefficiencies, as sales managers must now assume the primary duty of recruiting new employees. This can also prove to be a downward spiral, as the firm's reputation may become tainted as turnover rates increase, thus discouraging higher quality prospective employees from applying.

If the high turnover levels continue for quite some time, it causes tension with other employees as well. Employees in separate departments become discouraged by the turnover rate and constantly feel their job is in jeopardy as well, even though it isn't in most cases. The constant fear of job separation maybe a motivating factor to some individuals, but not most. I am reminded of a line in the movie *Glengarry Glen Ross:* "…'cause the good news is—you're fired. The bad news is…all of you've got just one week to regain your jobs, starting with tonight."

Funny movie; however, not incredibly motivational in my book. Intimidated employees may work better in the Marines than in financial services, and this was the environment of the aforementioned example.

If we look at correlations between the unemployment rate, asset values (like the S&P 500), and the Consumer Confidence Index (a measurement of spending and saving habits of consumers and generally accepted as an overall indicator of the mood of the economy), we find that unemployment rates have a dramatic influence on consumer confidence. This sounds like common sense, I know, but my interpretation isn't in regard to spending habits; it's the stress level and mood of your employees. If your asset values, such as the value of your home or 401(K), decline, your financial mood may decline, but not by a great deal. However, if your job or your income is in jeopardy, your financial mood deteriorates rapidly.

I point out this data not as an economic lesson, or analysis for that matter; it's just to aid in your communication, leadership and coaching of your employees. If an advisor is struggling to meet objectives, they are probably having financial difficulties as well, and threatening their job probably won't improve the situation. Instead, it will make them start looking for a new one. I realize that in our legalistic society, employers must give reasonable time for employees to correct performance deficiencies. A 90-day probationary period of corrective action may be an adequate tool in correcting an employee's minor transgressions. However, when you venture down the path of a financial professional whose primary objective is relationship building, it will be an obstruction to future performance as it strips them of any confidence moving forward with their clients and prospects. If the primary objective of this 90-day period is to "manage out" of an organization, you're better off offering a 90-day severance package and salvaging the clients before they can go elsewhere. The advisor will probably spend the 90 days looking for another position anyway. Of course, there may be other factors in place that make this scenario impossible. The point is not to use a probationary period as a corrective action tool and expect positive results.

A better alternative to the aforementioned scenario is to avoid the problems by preventing them before they occur. This sounds obvious enough, but I continue to be dumbfounded by the problems that surround certain institutions and the actions taken, and not taken, to correct them.

In another example, one organization asked me to look into a similar situation where they could not identify the failures of their wealth management platform. Over a period of seven years, the institution raised $300 million in AUM ($100 million from one investor), and approximately $100 million in brokerage assets. The total program revenue that year was about $1 million or $2 million below plan. The employee turnover rate for that period of time was an astounding 400%. In one region of 13 advisors, only one remained on the payroll.

My initial impression of this organization was that management was causing some type of unfavorable work environment, and so their employees were leaving. My assumption couldn't have been further from the truth. Management wasn't causing any negative work environment at all. In fact after being hired, most employees never spoke to their sales manager again until they were warned about substandard production. I realize that the term "micromanagement" is virtually taboo in the sense of management style, but this organization took the opposite approach to a similarly harmful extreme. Advisors were given tools and adequate resources, but no leadership, training or guidance whatsoever. The only successful advisor had survived by the attrition of his peers and inheriting their client relationships, which is probably not the best business model for growth.

Both of these organizational structures are what I like to refer to as "managing up." If you have a vertical management structure, meaning several layers of management, you should ask yourself if you manage up or down the chain of command. If you're a sales manager managing up the chain, then you have a true contradiction. How can you manage sales if your time is consumed by interactions with your supervisors? If your days are spent on budgets, meetings with supervisors or other department heads, and scheduling vacation days for your staff, I don't know that "sales manager" is the correct terminology. You are indeed a manager, but I don't think your endeavors are increasing sales. In fact, as in the above example, your primary job is recruiting.

I realize this may be an extreme situation, but I describe it to prove a point. In reality, most sales managers don't manage sales activities; they manage department processes. This is why I'm a huge advocate of hiring sales trainers and coaches in addition to department heads. Once a system is in place, someone needs to ensure that the policy and procedures are followed and objectives are met. Someone also needs to ensure sales are being monitored, activities are being tracked, and sales practices are being followed.

There are many tracking tools and activities that we will describe in detail in further chapters; however, they all require committed leadership. This is the job of a sales manager, coach, trainer or any other title you choose to use. Once roles are identified and proper employees are placed into those positions, you will see dramatic increases in production, substantially lower turnover rates, and, of course, higher shareholder value.

Another consideration when forming your practice is, of course, the budget. In today's world, cost-cutting seems to be the course of action that is "acceptable." Keep in mind that I do not condone excessive spending in any regard; however, I do feel that certain spending is warranted depending on the opportunities at hand and the desire to pursue them. I have seen so many organizations that arbitrarily spend funds with little regard to outcome. Traditional civic organizations, such as the local chambers of commerce and EDCs, are among them. Financial services firms will arbitrarily write checks to these organizations with no representation or quantifiable results. I realize that many of these contributions are made due more to civic responsibility than to business development. However, if you're going to spend the funds, shouldn't you get something beneficial out of the engagement? If not, perhaps the funds can be directed more effectively.

If dollars are spent, then results must follow. I am the first to admit that quantifying such expenditures can be a difficult challenge sometimes, but proper tracking can make the results easier to see. There is also the issue of "client entertainment" and "business development" expenditures. I have seen both sides of the extreme in these categories.

I was once brought into a moderately sized bank of approximately $5 billion in assets and was astonished at the fact they had not one, but two private planes for their executive officers. I realize that airports are an inconvenience, but really? That, of course, was in the heyday of the financial world. Today there are no first class tickets available, and if the trip's less than 500 miles, you're probably in a rental car with three co-workers and maybe sharing a room when you get there. In all reality, the extravagance wasn't used for business development; it was used because it was there. Reeling in the aftermath of "irrational exuberance," it's difficult today to get lunch with a high-end prospect covered through accounts payable.

I once did a proposal for a prospect in South Florida who spent summers in Seattle, Washington. It was a major client, so I prepared an in-depth analysis of his current holdings, made recommendations, and had everything bound together in a new leather binder. It was in July, so I flew to Seattle, stayed for four days, and made a formal presentation in front of a group of people that made the Spanish Inquisition look like a walk down Pike Street Market. At the end of the week I felt so out-classed by Harvard ties and an alphabet of impressive credentials that I limped my way back to Florida with a commitment of only $13 million, far less than the $100 million I was after. This was disappointing, but the big "win" was establishing the relationship. When I returned, I received accolades for building the connection, and was reimbursed the cost of the $75 leather binder— that's all. (Sometimes our cost-cutting endeavors get out of control.)

I had an accounting professor in college that referred to managers as "top line" or "bottom line" managers. I never liked the analogy, as it seems as though you give up one to obtain the other. The reference pertains to CEOs, department heads, and managers as to how you increase profit, or bottom line. Do you increase it through cost-cutting measures, such as reducing staff and other expenditures, thus creating more efficiency? Or by increasing sales and usually along with it, expenditure)? I suppose it depends on the type of organization you're running. Proctor& Gamble and Walmart grow exponentially by cutting cost, whereas top line growth can be challenging. Young companies focus more on top line revenue increases to add to the bottom line, regardless of cost. They see expenses as investments. This can present imbedded conflict with older financial institutions that have a cost-cutting mentality but a relationship-driven business.

Sales managers and program directors should propose that a portion of gross revenue be used for business development and retention, and, at the risk of alienating all the financial advisors out there, at the expense of the advisor payout. Now before all of you financial advisors throw this book out the window, consider a few things.

Client development expenditures must be allocated in the same way as other costs. As department heads, you've all seen that bill at the end of the year that includes allocation costs from non-revenue producing departments, or cost centers. This expense includes the cost of running the bank outside of your department and usually includes HR expenses, legal and compliance fees, and executive compensation that cannot be allocated towards specific departments. These are operational costs, necessary expenditures that keep the institution running. Certain local expenditures need to be accounted in the same way. A chamber of commerce membership benefits the entire institution at a local level and should be included in the general expenditures. However, when you take a client out for a round of golf or lunch, it may or may not benefit the institution as a whole, and should be accounted against specific department revenue.

Note the impact of "above the grid" accounting on an arbitrary financial advisor's commission grid. The expenses are not born by either the FA or the institution; rather, they are shared between the two benefitting parties in equal proportion.

This scenario still maintains above-average margins. In this example, there is no allocation for the cost of employee benefits, which may or may not be reflective in your cost center. That varies by institution and was deliberately excluded for this reason. This example is derived from an actual program using a third-party provider for investment services, charging an 11% fee plus ticket charges for their service. The sales assistant assumes either a shared entity or a subscription service. Other costs of the institution include sales management salaries and bonuses, plus administrative cost and taxes.

Unless your institution is completely sustainable and relies solely on cultivating existing clientele, you must be willing to spend dollars on business development and employee retention. I am not referring to being the named "platinum" sponsor for every event in town. You must analyze the opportunity and attempt to quantify desired results. A lunch for a client and his wife at the local diner may mean more then sponsoring the opera house's 25th anniversary party. Your advisors may not already have the mindset to do this cost-benefit analysis, but you can coach them, hold them accountable, and then trust them to know what makes the most sense.

	FA Production	Details
Financial Advisor		
Gross Dealer Concession (GDC)	30,000	
Allocation Cost	500	Benefits entire department
Business Development	1,500	FA Business expenses
Sales Assistant	1,000	Sales Assistant expense
Misc Expenses	0	
Net GDC	27,000	Net revenue from production
Financial Advisor Payout (35%)	9,450	Advisor payout 35% of net GDC
Department		
Program Revenue	17,500	Net GDC less FA payout
Clearing Costs (15% of GDC)	4,500	Estimate of TPP cost
Internal Expenses (20% of GDC)	6,000	Management expenses /other costs
Profit / Loss	7,050	Pretax department profit
Profit Margin	23.5%	Margin based on GDC

Chapter 3
DEFINE YOUR DESIRED CLIENTELE

Now that we have covered the critical step of defining one's business purpose, and how coaching and leadership must be available to the sales staff to keep morale (and productivity) high and turnover low, it's time for a *lesson* on how to define your ideal client profile. This is an exercise that advisors often talk about, but rarely expand on. I have had many business partners ask, "What type of clients are you looking for?" My response was usually, "someone with investable assets." Honestly, that's probably a good answer to an internal line of business partner, as you probably wouldn't turn down a referral from any source. However, when it comes to your own pursuits, who would you most like to have as a client?

Let's go back to our vision for just a moment and look at the common traits. In the example of the offshore loan closings, what did the transactions have in common? The loans were all sizable, so the individuals were wealthy, which is something most advisors are looking for. The hidden commonality is the *reason* they were there. These loans were all commercial, meaning all of the clients were engaged in some sort of business. Most were either the CEO or CFO of their respective companies, which were expanding, hence the reason for the loan. Most were also younger than the traditional investment client, and some were highly educated and very comfortable with investment terminology. By contrast, many local advisors specialize in working with retirees, which usually means they have different goals, a different lifestyle, and more limited knowledge of financial matters than the type of client I wanted to attract.

If your vision involves being the hero of the local retirement community, funding offshore loan closings may not be in your future. As we saw earlier, commercial banks have a wide array of products and services to offer clientele, ranging from free checking accounts to commercial loans. Your firm and the position you are in will obviously influence your focus.

Personalities also play a big role in attracting clients. I'm not going to go into too much detail about the studies done in the 1950s segregating type A and B personalities, as you've probably all taken a few personality tests during your career. However, one of the *lessons* I want to share with you is that you must be aware of these distinctions and take them into account. The theory describes type A individuals as ambitious, rigidly organized, and highly status-conscious. They can be sensitive, truthful and impatient. They will always try to help others, take on more than they can handle, and want other people to get to the point. They are proactive and obsessed with time management. People with type A personalities are often high-achieving "workaholics" who multi-task, push themselves with deadlines, and hate both delays and ambivalence.

In his 1996 book, *Type A Behavior: Its Diagnosis and Treatment*[1], Meyer Friedman suggests that type A behavior is expressed in three major symptoms: free-floating hostility, which can be triggered by even minor incidents; urgency and impatience, which causes irritation and exasperation (those with these traits are usually described as being "short-fused"); and a competitive drive, which causes stress and an achievement-driven mentality. The first of these symptoms is believed to be covert, and therefore less observable, while the other two are more overt.

The theory describes type B individuals as the near-opposite of those with type A personalities. People with type B personalities generally live at a lower stress level and work steadily, enjoying achievement, but not becoming stressed when they do not achieve. When faced with competition, they do not mind losing and either enjoy the game or back down. They may be creative and enjoy exploring ideas and concepts. They are often reflective, thinking about the outer and inner worlds.

After making an assessment of yourself, ask yourself how you would feel dealing with the opposite personality. In our industry, we have a tendency to assume that everyone is a type A personality, yet in reality, most people are not. In fact, type B personalities have a tendency not to get bogged down by adversity and cope better with certain issues beyond their control.

In the financial services industry, on an average day we see more curve balls than fast balls down the middle. We learn to expect the unexpected.

1 Meyer Friedman, Springer; 1 edition (October 31, 1996)

Not only do we deal with clients, but in today's world, we also deal with constantly changing regulations, operational nightmares, and the ever-present threat of merger or acquisition. The bulk of these issues are beyond the control of the front line sales executive, but somehow we're still supposed to have long term goals and a plan to achieve them.

A type B personality would be able to shrug this off with relative ease, whereas a type A may get bogged down in trying to fix the issues, which maybe a futile task. I explain this specifically so you will ask yourself what type of clientele you are most comfortable dealing with; however you must first accurately identify your own unique personality.

Dr. Tom Denham[2] characterizes professions with certain personality types; however, he breaks it down into A, B, C, and D personalities. It is useful to also consider these additional distinctions and better understand the personality aspect of your ideal client profile. Denham defines his four personality types as follows:

Type A "The Leader"

Behavior Characteristics: highly independent, take-charge, decisive, direct, business-like, ambitious, efficient, motivated, persistent, focused, risk taking, practical solution oriented, anti-routine, high-achieving, no-nonsense, multitasking, deadline driven and change oriented.

Weaknesses: aggressive, controlling, too competitive, impatient, status conscious, high strung, workaholic, prone to interruption, insensitive, overly fast-paced, easily upset over small things, blunt, rushed and time starved.

Appealing Jobs:

- Business

- Entrepreneurship

- Management

- Politics

- Many researchers believe that type A behaviors are a reaction to environmental factors and are influenced by culture and job structure. Many jobs today place unrealistic demands on time,

2http://blog.timesunion.com/careers/are-you-type-a-personality/982/

emphasize efficiency and productivity, and dole out heavy penalties for mistakes. This only creates additional stress, making people less patient. Others may be naturally intense, but this tendency is increased by environmental stress.

Type B "The Socializer"

Behavior Characteristics: highly extroverted, charismatic, easy-going, humorous, energetic, talkative, enthusiastic, gregarious, travel-oriented, community-minded, and attention-seeking.

Weaknesses: excessive socializing; may take things personally.

Appealing Jobs:

- Advertising

- Event planning

- Marketing

- Public speaking

- Sales

- Travel consulting

Type C "The Detailer"

Behavior Characteristics: introverted, accurate, logical, analytical, reserved, calculated, fact-craving, consistent, procedural, rule-abiding, predictable, dependable, loyal, patient, cautious, rational, risk-averse, deep, thoughtful, sensitive and precise.

Weaknesses: perfectionist, overly serious, conforming, uncommunicative, unassertive, excessively detail oriented and emotionally limited.

Appealing Jobs:

- Accountants

- Analyst

- Customer service representatives

- Engineers

- Programmers

- Technical careers

[I would add "physicians" in this type. They are detail-oriented and work such hard, long hours they often just want the facts and rationale behind your recommendations.]

Type D "The Distressed"

Behavior Characteristics: pro-routine, structured, orderly, dependable, supportive of others, punctual, consistent, motivated by security and benefits.

Weaknesses: anxious, angry, depressed, worried, tense, inert, change averse, unexpressive, low self-esteem, socially inhibited, uncreative; resists responsibility and prefers to be told what to do.

Appealing Jobs:

- Administrative assistants

- Clerks

As you look at this list, ask yourself: what type of client are you pursuing, and do you have an inherent personality conflict? Don't think you cannot do business across different personality types; you just need to change how you present yourself. Actually, if people have the same personality type, it may cause friction and make for a difficult relationship. If you're a true type A personality, a leader that basically tells people what to do, how well do you think you'll do with another type A, who may seek advice, but is subconsciously resenting being told what to do? They would much rather be informed and gently advised on what to do.

Adjusting to what works for them could be as simple as changing how you present your product: the difference between, "you need to buy life insurance to protect your family," and, "based on what you've told me, and your situation, I would advise this policy for this reason" may be the difference between having a new client, or not. Type A personalities have a tendency to surround themselves with B and C personalities. Ever heard the term "too many cooks in the kitchen?" This can translate into client/advisor relationships as well.

When considering your career path, these distinctions can also be quite useful. Have you ever worked at a firm that promoted the top producer into a management role? Sometimes, but not always, they don't do very well and often go back into a production capacity. Why do you suppose this happens? Even though many financial advisors would beg to differ, most are type B personalities. For some reason we seem to think of successful advisors as type A, but when we look at some of the characteristics, they're probably closer to a type B, as most of the characteristics listed define a sales role more than a leadership role. So if you take that personality and place them in a management/leadership role, we strip them of the exact attributes that made them successful in the first place.

Another way to utilize this list is when considering your centers of influence, or COIs. Connecting and building relationship with these people is one of the most effective uses of time and resources for an advisor. Thinking about your own personality and theirs can be helpful. I would add certain attorneys to the type C personality list; however, it really depends on their specialty. A district attorney with political aspirations would probably fit better in the type A category, whereas a trust and estate-planning attorney could be a C personality, as they are more detailed and analytical in their profession. So when courting COIs to help garner referrals, how do you act according to their chosen profession and possible personality types?

Early in my career, as most advisors do, I figured out that attorneys and accountants can be a wonderful resource for prospective clients. I would invite them out to play golf, attend charity events, or watch a baseball game. We always had a great time, as I am a B personality and I get along with everyone; however, I never got any referrals out of them. This was somewhat perplexing, as I thought I was doing the right thing. Everyone knew me, and I knew all the right players. However, nothing materialized. I seemed to be pushing the wrong buttons.

Then in February of one year, I began to receive the phone calls that every advisor loves to get just before tax time. The CPA or designee would call, asking for missing tax documents, cost biases on assets, trade confirmations, and whatever else was needed to complete a client's tax return. This was an annual rigmarole that had been occurring for the past 20 years. It was a pain, as the time it took generated no revenue, and in some cases it required a bit of research, potentially consuming most of the month. Then, one year, I decided to beat them to the punch. In January, when I had some time open, I compiled a list of my clients and their corresponding accountants. I sent out letters to the CPAs explaining that I was the financial advisor for Mr. & Mrs. Client, and if they needed any additional information in order to complete their tax returns, they should contact me and I would be happy to assist.

Sometimes we just fall into success. At the time, I wasn't keeping close track, but I can tell you that those 35 letters generated close to 80 referrals from seven different accounting firms—not just the individual CPAs that I already knew. Evidently, this was more of a pain for the CPA firms than it ever was for me, and my letter was the hot topic around the water cooler all the way up to tax time. I was getting referrals for accounts that I had never met. Evidently, most of the calls to other advisors went unreturned for weeks, and many never returned the call. When it was time for the accounting firm's client to come in and sign the return, my name usually came up.

The point to this story is that you need to know what buttons to push with different personality types and professions in order to garner quality prospects. The social environment that I was extremely comfortable in did little to entice results from a certain personality group, whereas helping these accountants at technical level paid great dividends. Matching your efforts to the needs of certain personality types is smart when dealing with COIs as well as clients, and the easiest way to ascertain what is appealing to them is simply to ask them.

A key point in this *lesson* is to consider the possible clientele that you would find in each category, whether or not you would like to do business with them, and how you would find them. When you look at the list, type A leaders would be an obvious target, as demographics would indicate they would have accumulated wealth. However, as I mentioned earlier, they can create an inherent personality conflict if not approached in the right manner. Type B personalities are probably very similar to you; in fact, I would say that the bulk of my clientele over the years have come from this sector. I met most of them through social interactions and have continued that relationship moving forward. They can be extremely strong advocates of your work and are an excellent source of referrals, considering they normally have a large group of friends and business associates. I have had the least success with type C personalities, but, as in the example of being of service to accountants and their clients, you can be successful if you're listening, and making the effort.

I once had a referral from a local attorney for a husband and wife, both of whom were engineers. I met with them on several occasions, got to know their needs and concerns, and was ready to make a recommendation. I had everything typed up and bound, with a table of contents, reference materials—you name it. I thought I was way ahead of the curve until the three-hour meeting, during which I explained my rationale behind the recommendation and answered questions. They were leaving on vacation the next day, so they wanted to take the material with them and make a decision when they returned.

About 10 days later they got back in town and booked an appointment with me to finalize the transaction. When they arrived at my office they each had their proposal books with them, and opened them up. They didn't only have a few questions about my recommendations; they each had each gone through the prospectus in fine detail, highlighting certain paragraphs and making notations all throughout the document, even scratching out items that they didn't "agree to" (and had done all of this while on a cruise to the Caribbean).

They actually turned out to be great clients over the years, but how many advisors would be willing to jump through so many hoops? And how many would want to? Garnering the type of clients that you enjoy doing business with isn't as hard as you may think. It's all really a matter of who you are targeting. You don't get to be that selective of your clients when working in a bank environment. You may get referrals from all demographic types, depending on the bank affiliation and branch location. This is one reason why understanding the personality types will help you as you work with such a variety of clients.

If you just look at the geographical area of the branches that you cover, you can probably accurately ascertain the type of clientele they cater to. Urban environments will be more concentrated with professionals, business clients, local governments and professional services, like attorneys and CPAs. Suburban environments would have more families and possibly retirees, even though the emergence of industrial and office parks has moved many jobs out of the cities and into the suburbs. When I look at my community and my marketing strategy, I note that I work in the heart of a city, surrounded by law firms, business headquarters and government agencies. My marketing plan is very different than those of my counterparts in the suburbs, where they are surrounded by golf courses and soccer fields; our daily encounters are as different as night and day. How you position yourself in your own particular environment will have an enormous impact on your success.

Chapter 4
POSITIONING YOURSELF

Have you ever noticed that certain people just always seem to be in the right place at the right time? Early in my career, I would speak with other advisors that seemed to have business just fall into their lap, and I would wonder why I never got that lucky. It seemed as though every piece of business that I brought in was a challenge and took a great deal of time and effort.

During a conversation I had with a top producing advisor in Cincinnati, Ohio, he revealed his secret to me. He told me that while, on any day, being struck by lightning was remotely possible, your odds of getting struck increase dramatically if you're on the golf course in a thunderstorm waiving a nine iron over your head. What he meant was that putting yourself in certain "favorable" situations increases your odds of getting struck. Sounds simple enough, but do you put yourself in the way of opportunities, or do you wait for them to appear?

During a meeting with a group of Business Development Officers at a local trust company, we were discussing the types of clients that we were all trying to attract. The criteria for their service were a liquid net worth over $1 million or $250,000 in annual income. When I asked one colleague the question of how many of these target prospects he encountered that week, he looked at me like I was from Mars. I wasn't talking about how many referrals he received, or clients that he spoke with, I just wanted to know how many millionaires he encountered that week during his normal walk of life. His response dumbfounded me: "I don't really hang out in that circle." Now, I understand that it's difficult to live like a millionaire without actually being one, but you may want to consider how likely it is to get struck by lightning if you never go out in the rain.

Once you ascertain the type of clients that would be a "good fit," you must position yourself in situations that attract those clients, which can vary greatly not only by your preference, but according to geographic and economic factors as well.

In my community, like many coastal communities in Florida, we have a lot of wealthy retirees that like to be entertained. We have a thriving arts community, too many golf courses to list, and yacht clubs within miles of each other, all filled to capacity. As a financial professional, how do you run in that circle if you don't have a 50-foot yacht? It's not as hard as it may seem—it's a matter of picking and choosing your activities and how you spend your time. You may not have a yacht, but you may be able to have lunch or dinner at a yacht club on occasion. I understand there are private clubs, but many are not. You've got to eat someplace, so start inching your way into another lifestyle.

In Florida, the opportune conversations are definitely at the golf clubs. More business is revealed and discussed on the 19th hole then anyplace I've ever seen. After a round of golf the topic of conversation usually just evolves into conversations about markets and politics (I would warn you to avoid the latter as you never know whom you're speaking with!). Even if you're not a golfer, you can lunch at the country club and find yourself becoming more and more comfortable around very wealthy people.

Another *lesson* here is that top producers are wealthy people, so get used to the lifestyle!

Don't limit yourself to thinking you have to spend like a millionaire right off the bat in order to be part of their circles. To fit in, yes, you should dress accordingly, but the most important thing you can do (and it doesn't cost any money) is to develop your conversational skills. Beyond the basics of being an attentive listener, you need to do some homework on what to listen *for*. Remember, initially you are seeking introductions, or are talking with an introduction with the idea they could become a prospect. We all know that just because someone fits our ideal client profile does not mean they will ever become a prospect, many times for reasons beyond our control (e.g., his wife is a CFP). So, one thing to listen for is any clue about where they currently get their financial advice.

Another key clue to listen for is any mention of a big life change or transition. These include divorce, imminent retirement, loss of parent or spouse, sale of a business, etc. Keeping in mind that you are not going to try and sell anything during an early conversation in a social setting, you should just focus on gathering clues. You should add these notes to the contact's information on your computer because they will be invaluable when you do get that sales appointment.

In keeping with the truism that we have two ears and only one mouth for good reason, your listening skills are critical. But what about conversational, relationship-building speaking? Very important, as well. There are volumes written elsewhere on communication skills, but one key for our purpose of positioning one's self among wealthy people (and fitting in) is to learn to speak the language.

Remember, at this stage your conversations are not (mainly) about bond yields and 401Ks, though these topics fit in with what high-net-worth people may think about and what you are comfortable talking about. At this stage, you are in a social setting and different (non-financial) jargon is appropriate. That's correct—learning the *jargon* is one of the smartest homework assignments you can give yourself in order to have productive conversations in social settings with wealthy people.

If you are a golfer, you already know the jargon to expect while lunching at the golf club. If you are not a golfer but you are going to be in a golf setting (the club or perhaps a charity tournament), you should at least be able to hear and speak basic golf talk, know who is leading in the Masters, and why the course you are at is named "Bobby Jones."

In another example, let's say your firm provides ballet tickets for you to give your prospect, which you appreciate because you know he and his wife love ballet but are too new to the area to already have season tickets. Sure, you could simply send them the tickets, but with a little homework (if you need it) you can talk about the particular event using a small amount of jargon, and connect with the prospect more on equal ground.

The *lesson* here is that positioning yourself includes not only where you are standing on the map, but where you stand in your conversational skills, i.e., knowing how to listen for clues, and how to speak the social language of wealthy people.

Chapter 5
THE SALES CYCLE

Now that you have defined your target clientele and positioned yourself in situations that create opportunities, what's next? The true sales cycle begins. For a moment, step into a room with me—it is full of well-dressed people standing around chatting while sipping adult beverages. Imagine walking up to a gentleman, cutting in on his conversation as smoothly as possible and asking him his name. Now imagine that instead, when you stepped into that room you were greeted by a close friend who led you over to the same man, and introduced you. Feels much better, easier, and more likely to result in a productive conversation—so the word "introduction" is the powerful, key term we'll use for what we want. (Remember "leads clubs" where people passed you names to cold call? These are not *introductions*.)

We will define the beginning of the sales cycle as the "introduction." You may have heard this referred to in different ways, such as "prospect" or "acquaintance." However, I feel that "introduction" is the initial phase of the sales cycle, so we'll begin there.

Now, of course, not everyone that you meet needs to be classified as an *introduction*, but I would err on the side of inclusiveness if only because it will help you in numerous ways. In later chapters, I'll show you some tricks for keeping track of your new database (your contact list on your computer), so for the sake of this chapter, just assume someone else is keeping track of everything. If you work for a bank, this introduction phase may be easier than in your wire house or independent counterparts, as most institutions have a compensation package in place to incentivize employees to make these introductions.

Perhaps you received an introduction from your COI network, or you met a fellow dad at little league practice. Regardless of the source, we begin the sales cycle as an introduction and **ITS SOURCE**. I don't mean to scare you with the caps and bold type, but noting the source of the introduction is such an important step, simply because it can be duplicated. So you now have an introduction and its corresponding source—perhaps a tablemate gave you their business card at a chamber of commerce breakfast. The next step, by the way, is where 90% of people fail—you must initiate contact within 24 hours. After that, they've probably forgotten about any conversation that you had.

You won't find many situations where I recommend the use of electronic communications, but this is one of them. You need to get some sort of correspondence out quickly, and email is a great way to do this. It doesn't need much content, just a simple "nice to meet you yesterday at breakfast." You also need to ask them a question, preferably about something you discussed, or maybe seeking their advice about something. For example, most people are happy to give you the name of their accountant, BMW mechanic, or other trusted resource which may relate to a topic from your conversation. Also, I have always used upcoming events as a means for continuing the conversation, asking them if want to have lunch, meet for happy hour, or even a free community or educational event. The type of invitation is dependent on the opportunities presented, but it should be conservative at this stage. Don't invite them to a high-ticket charity gala without getting to know them better and ascertaining the potential for a business relationship.

I realize that your organization may not have the budget to host or even take part in many events on a regular basis, but I feel that I lobbied pretty heavily in Chapter 1 as to the merits of social activities, and they don't need to be expensive. If you have no budget at all, which I have seen in certain large institutions, you may need to get creative, or start spending some of your own dollars if you feel it's a wise investment. Pay close attention to cost and be sure to account for the cost associated with the individual. Again, we must quantify everything, so keep track of the meetings and expenses.

So now you've had lunch with an introduction that you met at a chamber breakfast and have uncovered a possible opportunity regarding an old 401(K) that needs to be rolled over. I would not go into specific detail while in any social setting. Rather, use this as an opportunity to schedule a follow-up appointment at your office, or perhaps their home or office, if that would be more comfortable for them. You do, however, need to get some personal information in order to prepare for the follow-up appointment, most of which you may have gathered through the course of normal conversation. Simply inform the prospect that they'll be receiving a "pre-appointment packet" in the mail that is customarily sent out, and ask if you should send it to their home or office address. If they say their home, make sure you get the home address—it probably is not on their business card or web site like their office address would be. At this point, we also update the classification of this contact from "introduction" to "prospect." One way to know it's time to do that is to ask yourself what conversation you are now engaged in: when the conversation shifts from finding common ground and becoming acquainted to discussing actual potential ways they could do business with you, the status changes.

Now you're probably asking yourself, *what is a "pre-appointment packet?"* It is important that you send out a packet that is easy to read (i.e., no technical information) and isn't actually problematic if ignored. It includes three primary items:

1   Introduction Letter—A brief introduction to you and your firm with pertinent information, such as your name, phone number, and office address. Include the time and location of the scheduled appointment and a phone number in case a conflict arises.

2   Financial Advisor Bio—Most organizations have these prepared for their advisors, but in case they don't, write your own, but keep in mind that it must be accurate and approved before use. The bio normally lists your experience, educational background, civic affiliations, and perhaps some personal information, such as interests or hobbies. It actually looks a lot like your LinkedIn profile.

3   Agenda for Meeting—it's imperative that you include it, and in a particular format. As you see the example packet on the following pages, the first three items on the agenda are numbered, however, blank. The fourth number on the list is *your* agenda item—in this example, a 401(K) rollover. The first three are up to the prospective client, and you may be amazed at what they write down. Often they're things that you would never think to bring up, but are obviously important to the prospect.

SAMPLE: INTRODUCTION LETTER

Don Watson
XYZ Investments, Inc.
23 Main Street
Sarasota, FL 34236

[Date]

Dr. Charles XYZ
123 Ringling Boulevard
Sarasota, FL 34203

Dear Dr. XYZ,

Please allow me to introduce myself. My name is Don Watson and I am a Financial Advisor with XYZ Investments, a division of XYZ Bank. I understand that you recently opened a checking account with us and Mary Smith at the Main Street branch, and that we will sit down to meet next week to answer any financial planning questions you may have.

I look forward to our appointment scheduled for 11:00 on Tuesday at the Ringling office. I have enclosed my Bio information, as well as a meeting agenda. Note the top three items on the agenda are open so you can jot down anything you would like to cover during our meeting.

In order to provide the best possible advice, it is helpful if you bring along any financial statements that you may have. I look forward to meeting you.

Sincerely,

Don Watson
Financial Advisor

Enclosures (2)

SAMPLE: AGENDA FOR MEETING

XYZ Investments, Inc.

June 1, 2014

Agenda

1.

2.

3.

4. Review current financial plan

5. Current investments review

6. Review transitions and personal life
   changes which may have financial impact

7. Note next actions and schedule follow up

Now that you have a scheduled appointment and you've sent out the pre-appointment packet, hopefully your next encounter with this prospect will include a sale. This means the conversation has progressed from establishing relationship, through discussing potential opportunities to do business, to them making a commitment to at least one of your offers. For efficient and effective tracking, this path correlates to the designations of "introduction," "prospect," and "client."

This conversation (to turn your prospect into a client) is one with which you are already familiar, and hopefully skilled. This is actually the point that advisors are most comfortable with, and many have their favorite tried-and-true techniques that I wouldn't even attempt to change. Having said that, I'm still going to make a few broad suggestions.

Without too much time-wasting chitchat, ask them if they brought their agenda. If they did, they more than likely wrote something for the top items so it's evident where to start the conversation and you would be amazed at the content. It usually consists of other business opportunities, perhaps a maturing CD or large cash balance. I've seen it include a copy of their brokerage statement. If they didn't, hand them a copy (which of course you have with you) of what you sent them. This is your meeting agenda, and you should go through it along with your personal profiling questions.

Many advisors have entirely different methods of conducting this interview. Some use a computer and go through a list of questions, but I'm not a big fan of this method because it takes away from the human element uniquely available in a face-to-face appointment. Your prospect doesn't need you to type data into a terminal; they can get that on their own through numerous web pages and applications. I have always been a *yellow pad advisor*, meaning I take notes on a yellow legal pad; however, I also write directly on my agenda. As items are addressed or uncovered, they are either added to the agenda or marked as complete. These notes are important because they will be used later to write a summary of the meeting which will be sent to the client and also put in his or her file.

Financial advisors always seem to focus their attention on assets and the performance of those assets. Except those who have a strong insurance background, few ever touch on liabilities. I don't mean that in the traditional sense of financial planning. If you work for a bank, you may ask someone about their mortgage rate because you hope to uncover an opportunity to cross-refer to another department, but how many ask about auto insurance coverage? Not that I want to, or am able to sell auto insurance, but that issue could prove to be a major liability to your client, especially if there are teenage drivers involved. Discussing this could also lead to a COI relationship with a property and casualty insurance provider.

There are other issues which fall into the category of potential liabilities. Most advisors are aware of the impact of taxes, both income and estate. However, do you ask your 40-to-60-year-old client about their parents' financial well-being? If your clients are in that age bracket, they more than likely will have experienced some type of event regarding their parents, generally either an illness, move out of their home, or passing. This could prove to be financially draining and needs to be taken into consideration when planning. On the other side of this conversation, it could also uncover a possible inheritance, and maybe even generate a referral to the parents. These are the types of questions that open doors, and they need to be included into conversations when appropriate.

Now that you have completed the transaction and the former "prospect" is now a "client," are you done at this point? Do you now just hope that everything gets processed smoothly and that you'll only talk with the client again when they want to buy something additional? Of course not. The follow-through phase of the sales cycle is critical, yet something that is rarely completed, as it's not exactly easy to do so. If executed properly, however, it will strengthen the new relationship and even uncover more current opportunities to do business.

The follow-through phase occurs within a few days of the initial transaction, usually the opening of the account. At the risk of all the financial advisors reading this and screaming a collective "WHAT???" it's important that I address this next phase.

A phone call needs to be made to the client welcoming them to the institution and ensuring that everything went as expected with the transaction. This call needs to be made by someone with a title—not necessarily your boss, but someone with a perceived level of authority. This works great with banks, as many have either local or regional presidents. If you don't have that luxury, your sales manager will do just fine. It gets a little more difficult at a wire house, and even harder if you're an independent advisor, as you may be the only employee at your location.

The point of the call is to engage the client through a different perspective, and ask a scripted set of questions designed to uncover potential opportunities. I actually presented this concept to a bank program based in Alabama, and it worked so efficiently, it was actually implemented by the retail arm of the bank. Every new relationship received a follow-up call from an officer at the institution. The level of officer was decided through a coding mechanism when opening the account. If the banker felt this client had the potential to become a major relationship, the local bank president made the phone call; if the likely outcome was a smaller account, perhaps the branch manager would call. The point is that someone reached out and said "thank you for your business," gave them a secondary contact number, and made certain that their needs were met.

For any compliance officer reading this, I am aware of the issue of having a non-licensed person calling on new brokerage clients. I assure you that it is a scripted call and doesn't involve product conversations whatsoever. This is an example of an actual script used by the local city president of a bank.

Caller/ Assistant:	Good evening, may I speak to Dr. Gordon, please?
Dr. Gordon:	This is Dr. Gordon.
Caller/ Assistant:	Hello, sir, this is Mandy, and I have Don Watson, the city president of XYZ Bank, on the line, and he'd like to speak with you for just a moment. Would you have some time for him?
Dr. Gordon:	I would. Philip [my financial advisor] said he would be calling.
Caller/ Assistant:	Thank you, sir. I'll put him through.
City President:	Dr. Gordon, this is Don Watson. I'm the city president of XYZ Bank in Sarasota. How are you this evening?
Dr. Gordon:	Very well. Philip mentioned that you may be calling.
City President:	That's great! He is one of best and brightest here at XYZ, and we're lucky to have him. I just have a couple of questions for you if you have a few minutes. Would that be okay?
Dr. Gordon:	Yes, that's fine.

City President:	I trust that all went well with your transaction with Philip, no surprises or anything?
Dr. Gordon:	All went well. I'm very happy.
City President:	That's wonderful. May I ask what brought you to XYZ bank?
Dr. Gordon:	We recently retired here to Florida and I had a CD due at (Any town) National. Their renewal rates were lousy, so I thought I'd check here since I drive by here all the time. Yours aren't much better, but Cathy referred me to Philip and said he may be able to do a little better.
City President:	Well I'm glad he could help. Let me ask you, is Anytown National your primary bank?
Dr. Gordon:	It is. We have a checking account there, as well as few other CDs.
City President:	Do you maintain your investments there as well?
Dr. Gordon:	No we have those at (Big Broker) Institutional.
City President:	Are you happy with the service that you're getting there?
Dr. Gordon:	It's been sporadic…our advisor left about a year ago and someone else took over the accounts, but I rarely hear from him.
City President:	Oh that's too bad. I'm sure you discussed that issue with Philip at your meeting.
Dr. Gordon:	Actually, not very much. I mentioned that I had some other investments, but we really focused on that maturing CD.

City President:	That's fine. However, if it's okay with you, I think I'm going to bring that up to Philip and have him get back to you on that. It's important that you have communication with your advisors. You mentioned that you're recently retired. What do you and your wife like to do? The reason that I ask is that we periodically get tickets to local events and I'd like to pass them on if you have an interest.
Dr. Gordon:ww	That would be wonderful! We enjoy the symphony and the ballet, and I love to play golf.
City President:	Perfect. I'll see if I can get you out sometime soon. In the meantime, I'm going to have Philip get back to you regarding those investment accounts and see if we can do a better job for you. If you need anything, don't hesitate to give me a call.

Now, I realize that "Dr. Gordon" is a very cooperative client, and this example may not always be the norm. But, this actual script was used by a city president to call all new accounts opened in the region, and the results were nothing less than outstanding. The list eventually got too large and we had to segregate the list to other officers in the bank. Please note a few important items: this is a formal call, introduced by an assistant. The intent is for the client to perceive the caller as someone of importance, which is why city and area presidents work well, given their titles. If the call is being made by a department head, "director" works well too. That five minute call will leave a lasting impression on that client, and your hope is that he will relay that message to his golfing buddies.

The call, as scripted, usually uncovers some additional key information about the client. In the example, we found out about bank accounts and CDs at Anytown National, and his brokerage accounts at Big Brokerage Institutional, and we got permission for Philip to follow up. I'm not saying that Philip's work was lacking to miss these things; perhaps time just got in the way, but either way, some new opportunities were uncovered and a relationship was solidified. Not bad for a five minute follow-up call.

This follow-up time needs to be blocked off on the calendars of higher ranking employees within an organization. In a bank environment, it seems the higher up the chain of command you go, the less contact you have with clients. These calls can be done in about an hour a week, given a typical number of active and new clients, and can produce phenomenal results. Also, the president or director needs an easy and fast way to communicate back to the advisor the results of the call. Then the advisor must contact the client, within 48 hours, to follow up as promised. This follow-up system, once in place, will quickly become a clearly justified use of upper management as well as a smart way to expand opportunities for advisors.

The point of the call is to engage the client through a different perspective, and ask a scripted set of questions designed to uncover potential opportunities.

Chapter 6
THE ART AND SCIENCE OF REFERRALS

Over the years there have been many articles written about the affluent clientele and how they managed to land at the firm in which they conduct their business. Although the numbers vary by years, it amazes me that generally over 80% of them do business with people they know personally, or were referred by someone they know personally.

Some of the larger banks and brokerage firms have done some extensive research on their clientele's job approval rating of their advisors, and have come up with some interesting results. Generally speaking, the job approval ratings hover around 60%, which is the higher end of the curve—very few came in below 50%. However, I would attribute that to other circumstances. For instance, if your approval rating of an advisor is in the 30% range, you would probably just get a new advisor and not remain a client of the institution.

Brokerage firms came in much higher in satisfaction ratings scoring in the mid 70% to 80% range, as did smaller community and regional banks. When I looked at all the data surrounding the ratings, a few items stood out. Full service brokerage firms and community banks have a tendency to have considerably more "touch" when dealing with their clients and may have personal relationships with many of them, whereas a large scale regional or national bank may have thousands of clients, most or even all of whom have never formally met anyone in the institution.

A large regional bank in the Eastern United States reported that 30% of their customers came into the branch only once to open their account and have never returned, and 40% utilized the branch facility just one time per year. That's 70% of their clientele who come into the branch less than once every 12 months. That doesn't give a great deal of time to build solid relationships and create high job approval ratings. In fact, I would speculate that the rating is based more on the non-human encounters, like ATM machines and online banking.

Even with the seemingly dismal approval ratings at many banks, when high-net-worth customers were asked if they would refer a client to their financial services institution, amazingly, 80% said yes, they would. When asked if they had, though, 90% of that group said they had not.

If you are a typical banker and have 100 clients at an average commercial bank, 60 of them think you're doing a good job, 80 of them would give you a referral (even though only three-fourths of the group think you're doing a good job), and yet only eight of them have given you one. Why do you suppose that is? Here's my theory: we have a career that involves speaking with individuals about very personal matters. I would venture to guess that speaking to people that you may not know very well about finances would rank second after health issues in the "it's none of your business" category. (In some retirement-aged communities like Sarasota, Florida, financial matters are probably *first* on the list—health issues are a general topic of conversation and often times are brought up when you least expect it.)

It is important to appreciate the fact that even your best clients, your biggest fans, may be happy to endorse you but just are not going to find themselves talking with their friends about money. Perhaps they are still heeding the rule most all of us learned as children—don't ask people about their finances. I can remember being a small child and asking my father how much money he made, and was told that was a very rude question and impolite to ask. Come to think of it, it's somewhat amazing that I ever got into this field, considering.

Because all sales professionals want to be recommended by others and referred business, there are countless books, seminars and systems about referral generation, and I've seen many of these. Maybe some of them worked, because I do get plenty of referrals, but I can tell you that it hasn't been as simple as "just ask everyone" —advice I heard from a sales manager many years ago. There is a definite technique to the art and science of referral sourcing, and much of it depends on planning, a little forward thinking, and available capital resources.

I once met with a successful financial advisor who told me the story of his longtime, highly satisfied client, who, despite many requests, would not introduce him to his network of friends, more out of shyness than anything else. During one of their quarterly appointments, his client mentioned that he and five of his golfing buddies were headed to Canada for a fishing expedition. The advisor, being inquisitive as always, asked where they planned to stay and the dates of the trip. He proceeded to contact the lodge and ask what type of fishing lures his clients should be using that time of year. When the client arrived, there were six shiny new lures waiting for the client and his buddies. I don't know all of the details, but I doubt this cost the advisor more than about $30, and what did he gain? Even if the client's guests never did business with him, he made a great impression on his longtime client for minimal cost. And guess what? When the group returned from their trip, within one month, three of the five guests opened accounts with the advisor. This is great example of how to be creative in referral prospecting.

Thankfully, not all clients are shy about telling others they actually do have wealth to manage, and will pass on the name of their trusted advisor. Just as you needed to define your ideal client, it is a great idea to pay attention and understand your *ideal referrer*. If you do not do this already, be sure

A customized gift takes more thought than expense, and serves to cement the relationship and open doors of opportunity.

and write down the source of any new prospect or client. This information gives you the power to focus your efforts, time and resources. If you have the time and budget to take someone to lunch this week, wouldn't it make sense to extend the invitation to the person who just referred you the seventh client in less than one year? Another way to utilize that information is to note all the characteristics of the people who refer business to you. Are many of them CPAs? Small business owners? Yacht club members?

It is always an eye-opening exercise to look at your referral sources. You will discover key information so you can better follow up with people who are recommending you, thank them, and also do something to help them whenever possible. You could attend their favorite charity event (be sure to sit at their table) or, if a referrer is a business owner, one of the very best ways to grow your relationship is to refer business to them. Remember, relationship-building activities with a prospect or client may only ever result in *one* client account; a solid, mutually beneficial relationship with an ideal referrer can be the source of ongoing referrals and *many* accounts.

One side benefit of helping your clients develop the habit of referring people to you is that if you like dealing with certain clients, you'll probably like their friends as well; people trend towards similar personality types.

With the advent of social media, especially LinkedIn, you can research and find your ideal clients, and then get introductions to them through your social media network. The scope of this book does not cover all the ways to use social media for prospecting, but you should become knowledgeable and invest time joining LinkedIn Groups, for example, where you can develop relationships with ideal referrers. Of course, our compliance departments haven't exactly caught up to the ongoing trend towards social media, so make sure that you check with them first, as interpretations of regulation vary considerably from firm to firm.

Ideally, your referrers will find it easy to refer business to you. One, because they know you and trust you enough to feel comfortable recommending you; and secondly, because they are already talking with *your* ideal customers! This is why CPAs who work with high-net-worth clients are often ideal referrers. You are not competitors because you offer different services, but you are helping the same type of client in the same area of their life. Take time to identify what professional types also sell to your target market.

Your ideal referrer may not have a similar business at all, as in the example of a florist who has customers often walk in who are referred from the banker next door. She simply had a good experience as a customer with that banker and has an easy opportunity to send people next door, and he reciprocates. The mutually beneficial relationship is easy, cost-free and quite productive.

In addition to asking yourself what professionals already work with your ideal client type, you can further refine your ideal referrer profile. Is your ideal referral source local? Are they relatively young and technology-immersed? Are they new and hustling for business, or well-established as the most trusted brand in town? Once defined, the key to success with referrals is to answer this question: *How can I meet and gain credibility with those people?*

The answer begins by asking yourself another question: *What can I do for them?* As mentioned, learn what is important to them and make the effort to go to that fundraiser, or get them the baseball tickets, or introduce them to people who meet their ideal client profile.

An older method of referral prospecting involved the use of Client Advisory Boards. When banks began consolidating, this process seemed to fade in popularity, however given the right environment, it can still garner excellent results. Back in the day before the mega banks of the world, community banks ran the show. They were run by a Board of Directors, the same as today. As they got bigger, the Board became less and less involved with the client, so advisory boards were created.

This is nothing new to organizations as a whole as many nonprofit entities are governed by their respective boards, and advised by advisory boards. The board that I am referring to represents the consumer of your organization and their primary responsibility isn't profit margins, shareholder value, or compliance and regulation—it's all about sales. Why would a professional in your market donate maybe two hours a quarter to your cause? I have seen paid advisory boards but I don't think the members were there for the $250 per board meeting. There may be several reasons, but I can promise two of them are that it makes them look better in the community, and it may open doors for them to your firm's clientele.

When you consider the formation of a board like this, you must take into consideration the individuals that you are soliciting. Don't just think of how you can benefit, this will lead to a quick turnover of board members, think of how they can benefit first. Let's take a look at a few professions that may make good board members.

Attorney—	Probably room for two types of attorneys, such as real estate, business or trust and estate planning.
Accountant—	I would have just one accountant.
Real Estate Broker—	Provides access to new arrivals to the area.
Business Owner—	The entrepreneurial influence; can be leader in networking.
Real Estate Developer—	Probably well known in the community.
Minister—	Trusted community leader.

Depending on your own network, of course, you may have other professionals who you think would want this opportunity. Be sure and present your board member invitation as an opportunity for them as well, not like just a favor to you. Successful people are busy, but if they see this as a good use of their time, they will jump on board. One other tip to remember is that with today's technology advantages, you can have your board meet in person less frequently, perhaps only once a quarter, but meet at least once a month via conference call or video conference.

In these ways, developing your business through referrals is both an art and science: the science includes analyzing your current referral sources, specifying the characteristics of your ideal referrer, and systematizing your activities to increase referrals; the art of referrals is your ability to have people like and trust you. Period.

Chapter 7
TIME AND RESOURCE MANAGEMENT

During my years as an economics major at the University of Cincinnati, I had a specific class that focused on resource utilization. It was a class mostly about manufacturing and maximum capacity, and involved many of the topics I still rely on today. It's a pretty basic concept: take any business, say a restaurant open for breakfast, lunch, and dinner, and assume you turn your 150 seats three times per meal. That's 450 plates times three, or 1350 meals per day, seven days per week, 365 days per year. If you do the math, that's 492,750 meals per year, and at $15 per meal, that's about $7.4 million in revenue. This number is your maximum capacity, meaning it must be enough to cover all costs and make you a profit.

You would be amazed at how many startup businesses have higher operating costs then their maximum capacity. Of course, a typical restaurant would never come close to these numbers, but the point is to say this is the most that can be done under the given restraints. The only way to increase revenue without increasing the size of the facility is to increase your prices. The other factors are pretty much set in stone.

As advisors, the one resource that we have equal to everyone else is time. It is irrelevant how successful you are, what kind of car you drive, or what country club you belong to; we all still have just 24 hours in a day, and only 365 days in a year.

I use the economics concepts of maximum capacity to monitor my daily activities. Businesses use this same concept in the form of wages. If we base everything on an eight hour day, you can easily find your "value" to your organization. If I produced $500,000 in revenue last year, we just divide that by a 2,000 hour work year, or $250 per hour to your company's top line revenue. It makes a pretty strong argument for the use of sales assistants that cost 1/10 of that, but that's a different issue. I have a different concept than the traditional method, and some may say it's a bit demented. I really don't separate my work life from my personal life, as I feel they are very much intertwined. So instead of the traditional 2,000 hour work year, I have expanded it to equal maximum capacity, or an 8,760 hour actual year, and instead of dividing it by last year's production, I divide by the target production for the upcoming year.

So if your goal is $1 million in production next year, you only have 8,760 hours to get there. What this does is quantify all of your time, so you better get the most out of every hour, since they're each costing you $114. You do have to be very careful using this analogy, or else you'll find yourself avoiding all activities that produce no revenue, some of which you should, others of which you shouldn't. You can use this method to live each moment to the fullest, even if you're not measuring them in terms of literal dollar return-on-investment. If I'm going to spend three hours at my son's little league game, I'm going to get my $342 worth, meaning I'm going to be engaged and enjoy it. As for other activities, like surfing the web, watching reality TV, or updating Facebook, we might be more likely to cut down on that time.

This method is fairly simple with financial advisors, since virtually everything is related to gross revenue production. It's a little more difficult with someone like a private banker or Trust BDO, who may or may not have quantified goals. If this is the case with your situation, I would recommend indexing your goals. If you're a private banker and your annual goal is $10 million in AUM, $5 million in loans, and $5 million in deposits, it's difficult to project revenue in each category due to many variables, including when the business was booked, how long deposits remain, and the speed of loan repayments. Most of these issues are beyond your control, which is why most institutions don't compensate on actual revenue, but rather some type of point or scoring system. I would recommend using whatever that system is to calculate an hourly rate, using 100% as "meeting" your goals.

Now that we know how much an hour is costing us, how do we use the time and knowledge to our advantage? A private banker friend of mine happened to belong to the same country club that I belonged to, and one afternoon over lunch we were having a conversation about the number of clients that each of us had garnered from club affiliations. I was shocked by his results— in 12 months, not one client, not even for a checking account or credit card application. He was spending a fortune playing golf there a few times a week, dining there every Wednesday evening, and even attending the members' private functions. To my surprise, he also played in a Wednesday morning golf league that I played in, but I was unaware of his involvement.

Actually, his *lack* of involvement at the club turned out to be precisely the problem. He showed up—but that is not the same as becoming involved. It wasn't until months later that I realized that he always played golf in the same foursome, had dinner with his family on Wednesday evening, and basically sat in the corner with a drink at the member events. Literally

surrounded by potential ideal clients, he seemed to be waiting for them to approach him and start a conversation about their banking needs.

In particular, the concept of playing rounds of golf with your brother and best buddies on Wednesday morning dumbfounded me. I understand the concept of leisure time, but it's probably better to do that on a weekend then try to justify it as a business opportunity. I played in the same golf league as this banker, only I always opted for open play, meaning the league leader would set the groups. He also knew that my intent was to meet new people, so I was generally paired with someone I didn't know ,allowing for introductions and a few hours of conversation. The point to this story is that just because you belong to a country club or a charity board doesn't mean you can just sit back and wait for the phone to ring. You have got to be well known at the organizations you're involved in.

A golf course is just another branch office. Get to know your walk-ins.

With acute awareness of the value of your time, think about how any given hour could be most productive. That is how Top Producers think. One caveat must be mentioned: this is not an endorsement of the unattractive practice of turning every single conversation into a sales prospecting call. You are already successful and artful enough in your relationship-building skills to understand this, but it wouldn't hurt to review what we covered previously about how to converse with "introductions" and not get into specific opportunities until an appointment is set for that purpose. Then you have full permission and won't be "that guy" at the club who annoys people with his sales pitch when they would rather be talking tarpon, tuna, or tees.

Chapter 8
MAKE YOUR CRM SING

I would be willing to wager that nearly all financial professionals have tried a client relationship management, or CRM, system. If you have perfected its use, use it every day, and live by it, congratulations, you're in the under 20% category. Most advisors get one day of training, head back to the office, try it for a day or two, and for some reason find it too cumbersome to use. The complaints that I've heard are countless and diverse to say the least.

If you're one of the lucky ones who has an integrated system between the financial institution and the CRM, then you're already way ahead of the game since your contacts should already be in the system, saving you a ton of data entry. The downside is that most of those internal systems aren't exactly state-of-the-art. I've seen financial institutions that have three CRM systems, each running independently and unable to communicate with each other. Obviously, this is a problem.

In order to get started with this chapter, as I do in most situations, I will attempt to define our objective, or vision. In this situation, what would a perfect CRM system look like? My vision is a preloaded client information database that can be accessed through virtually any means of electronic or verbal communication. I would like to see records of conversations, emails, meetings, and personal events that don't stop with birthdays and anniversaries, but also may include a client's granddaughter's piano recital and his upcoming fishing trip to Alaska.

To access this useful information as I am preparing to talk to a client (thereby refreshing my memory and giving myself a personal edge), one thing has to be in place—the information! Being the social sales guy that I am, I don't spend a great deal of time behind my desk, which would be the ideal location to sit and update client files. However,

I'm usually out of my office when talking with clients, and as much as I would like to have a memory like a steel trap, I don't anymore.

If I could update a client file just by speaking into my phone, that would be wonderful. While driving between branches, I could be making notes of my last client meeting. As long as I can do that, why not schedule our next appointment, and make a mental note to call my mother? All of you with iPhones are probably saying this sounds a lot like Siri, and you're not wrong; as far as updating a calendar and making a phone call, "she" is wonderful. Just keep in mind that Siri doesn't actually book anything for you. She just updates data and takes instructions. If wanted to send a letter out to a client, or flowers to someone that just lost a loved one, Siri won't do that.

There are countless dictation software programs and a few companies that allow for voice instruction. Some of them use a computer program for the dictation; others use live personnel, many in foreign countries that can update data within 24 hours. The program dictation is generally in real time, but can cause some issues with strong accents or speech variances. A few years ago I had a supervisor with a deep southern accent that couldn't use Siri at all. Every time he would ask her for directions, she responded with "the nearest McDonald's is five miles away" (I guess Siri isn't a southern girl).

The system that I envision is one that updates files within minutes, not days, and is screened for grammatical errors and spelling. I want it to easily differentiate between a note for a client, and instructions to perform a task. So picture yourself leaving an appointment—you get into your car and hit a button on your smart phone. You state the name of the client or prospect, and just speak your mind. You go through the conversation and note the most important things, you schedule a time to follow up, or perhaps you need to run a proposal or variable annuity hypothetical. Maybe you just want to make a note that the client's son is playing in the high school state championship game and you need to check the score tomorrow.

Now with the perfect CRM system, all of this would be transmitted via a voice file and transcribed. All notes associated with the client would be entered into the "notes" tab and instructions would be carried out. By the time that you arrived back at your office, an email would be waiting asking for more information for the proposal, and the next morning you would have a news update of the championship game showing your client's son hitting a homerun to win it. Now you tell me if you think this information is valuable. I think it is, and it was all done with the touch of a button.

CRM systems are made to capture all sorts of data. Most users use them to capture financial data, but they are extremely useful in other aspects. This is where I update the source of my client, their interests, hobbies, family, friends, advisors, and just about anything else you can think of. As you continue to use the system, you'll find yourself with an incredible source of information at your fingertips. Just imagine your sales manager coming out and saying they have six tickets to the opera for the opening night performance. If only you knew anyone that loved the opera, it would be a great opportunity for a little social bonding. With your well-maintained CRM, you can know in a flash everyone in your database you have previously noted as opera goers. Make a call to a long time client and ask him to invite another couple. You never know what you may get out of it. Imagine how much energy and brain space that will be freed up if you let your system remember everything for you. You may think you know all the golfers, for example, but with your system you can have a complete list at your fingertips.

For many years, financial professionals have gone through a routine of sending out birthday and holiday cards to their clients. The enthusiasm usually fades over time, as more pressing issues present themselves. The thing that we sometimes overlook, especially in Florida, is that among our aging population we have many people with a very limited amount of contacts.

I had an 85-year old client that had lost his wife 10 years earlier. He explained that it was difficult since they had been together very happily for quite some time, and he was lucky to have the support of his family and friends throughout the experience. Then he proceeded to tell me that the worst part about getting older is that everyone you care about eventually passes on. Sadly he said that all of his friends and siblings had already passed. He did have children and grandchildren that lived out of state and he would see them on holidays, but really no one locally. I point out this story to emphasize the importance of reaching out to all of your clients, and not just at holiday time. The birthday card that you send out maybe the only one they get. Your CRM system should make this a piece of cake for you.

Having and maintaining a powerful CRM system provides your clients with added value, as I've described in the examples of social invitations, free tickets, and the sense of being known and connected. A CRM system adds value to you directly by not only helping to foster strong, long-term business relationships, but also it will significantly reduce the stress associated with being disorganized, under-informed, and seeing things fall through the cracks just because you could not personally attend to all the details. The *lesson* here is that investing in your CRM is not optional, and you can have it be more effortless than you may have imagined.

Chapter 9
IS YOUR HOUSE IN ORDER?

Before you venture down your new road to success in the financial services industry, I would like you to consider whether your own house is in order. I don't mean whether your lawn is mowed and closets are organized, what I mean is, how is your personal life going?

The financial sales business is a tricky one to say the least as the financial professions rank in the top 10 careers leading to depression and the top 20 in alcoholism. If you're not careful, downward spirals can happen virtually overnight. There's not much about this business that isn't stressful. We have to talk to strangers on a regular basis, ask a lot of personal questions like "how much money do you make," convince them that they need our advice, give them confidence to act on that advice, and possibly be wrong in the process. What's stressful about any of that? Add to that the enormity of the industry, its constantly changing regulation, consolidation of financial institutions, revenues getting squeezed to the lowest levels in history, and a sometimes very sporadic income, and you have the makings of a heart attack.

At the start of the economic meltdown of 2008, I was receiving $1 million per day in margin calls. 2008 was one of the best years I've ever had in new assets under management; unfortunately, the accounts were declining at a faster pace than new funds were coming in, and within a year, my book was cut in half. The Dow went from about 12,000 in March of 2008 to under 7,000 just one year later.

My clientele was not angered at me personally, as they all knew the risks associated with financial markets, but they obviously were not happy with the decline in asset values. As an advisor, you do the best that you can to comfort your clients and mitigate risk, but there's only so much you can do. At that time, my own house was in disarray as well. My personal investments were faring just as poorly as everyone else's, my home value had declined by 50%, and the biggest issue (due to the nature of fee-based investment advisory) was that my income was cut in half as well. Now, granted, the Great Recession was an anomaly and an extreme example of a stressful situation. However, financial advisors, trust officers, private bankers, and lenders all have their ups and downs, and much of their income is dependent on fluctuating asset values beyond their control.

Now, I would like to point out that I am not a health professional, therapist, physical trainer, or nutritionist, but I'm still going to give you a few hints on a few personal topics to get your own house in order. I don't know about you, but I have a tendency to perform better when things are going well. When I feel good, I stand up straighter, I speak with a purpose, and I'm considerably more confident and motivated to succeed at whatever I'm doing. When my pants are feeling a bit snug, everything seems a little harder to do, and I don't have the energy or motivation to go above and beyond. Now, I'm not saying that if you're overweight you can't be successful. What I am saying is that being healthy engenders better work habits, gives you more energy, and can boost your confidence. A *lesson* all Top Producers learn (some sooner than others) is that practicing self-care is not optional if you want to be ready and available to seize every opportunity presented. So, having said that, here are my four keys to a healthier you.

1. Remember this Simple Equation
   Calories in − Calories out = ?
   If positive, weight gain. If negative, weight loss.

2. Don't Drink your Calories

   A typical daily calorie intake goal (with adjustments depending on your age, weight, activity level and goals) is roughly 2000 calories, total. What and when you eat is key because no one feels like working if they feel faint with hunger or at the low end of a sugar high. You want your 2000 calories to nourish you but also give you a steady amount of energy and sense of feeling full enough to never be interrupted by a growling stomach. (This amount is for weight maintenance—the goal may temporarily be closer to 12-1500 if weight loss is the goal.) If 30% of your calories are ingested in liquid form, it's a recipe for disaster, in part due to what you are consuming. A shocking number of people out there will consume 600 calories from soft drinks alone (about four cans of regular cola). Some people think they are being smart by avoiding soda, but just one good old SMALL chocolate shake from McDonalds has 560 calories; or perhaps you're a Sonic drive-through fan, in which case you'd get 620 calories in that little treat. These are the "good" examples, by the way, as most adults have moved on to other, more potent beverages. Beer drinkers win the prize. A 12-ounce Budweiser packs about 145 calories, while its lighter counterpart saves you only 35 calories at 110. You may think this is far better than the Mickey D's chocolate shake, but you need to honestly ask yourself—do you ever have just one? It's kind of like a potato chip…*one* wouldn't be so bad, but…

Wine drinkers can be saving or squandering their calorie budget, depending. A glass of Merlot comes in at 120-150 calories, and one with dinner is not bad at all. A bottle between 5PM and bedtime—not so much. You also need to consider that these really are empty calories, as there's little nutritional content to any alcoholic beverage. I have spoken with many advisors that routinely have five to six beers on a normal evening; one even had a Kegerator at his home. That's 870 calories from light beer, and if you're a Dogfish Head kind of guy, over 1,700 calories, plus you probably couldn't stand up later. Hopefully, you get the point. We have about 2,000 calories to work with every day, and it has to supply you the energy all day long and keep you healthy in the process.

3. Don't eat after 8PM

Most nutrition experts would say 6PM, but I'm a realist. I rarely get home before 6PM, let alone have dinner. If you have a family and responsibilities, it's hard to have everyone where they need to be and done eating by 6PM. The point is not to eat so late the food doesn't have time to digest. If you're still eating at 9PM, it will just sit in your stomach and, some experts will tell you, turn into fat. Plus, it makes you feel horrible, sleep poorly, and makes it hard to get out of bed the next day.

I would expand this rule not only to food, but anything with calories. The concept is to fast in the evening hours, when you are generally least active. Another benefit to adopting this healthy habit is that you will avoid a large percentage of "unconscious eating" which usually occurs in the evening.

When a person is not alert and may be watching a television show, the next thing they know is they've eaten an entire bag of cheddar popcorn (900 calories, 540 of them from fat).

4. You can't "work off" a bad diet

Unless you're Michael Phelps or some other young professional athlete, do not think for one minute you can eat a terrible diet and then easily control your weight through exercise. With a poor diet, it's very easy to pack on pounds that you don't have time to burn off. Even if you have the physical ability and inclination, you probably don't have two extra hours every day to spend at the gym.

Watching what you eat is more important than anything. If you think I'm joking, here are a few examples of eating "pretty well." In this page from a food diary, we start out great at breakfast with a bowl of oatmeal and some fruit. I only use Applebee's only because there's one next door and it's usually packed for lunch. I asked the manager what their top-selling item was; to my surprise, it was a "Cowboy Burger." I had assumed it would be something lighter, especially at lunchtime, even though many of those "salads" are misleading. Now, you probably don't order a pizza every night, but I'm sure Papa John's or Domino's makes it through your door on occasion. The Ruffles potato chips are thrown in there, well, because I love them. You can keep your sweet snacks and soft drinks, but a bag of Ruffles doesn't stand a chance in my house—which is why there are none in my house.

You can see at the bottom of the diagram that we've consumed 2,866 calories. Forget about the nutritional deficit from consuming 124 grams of fat, just consider that this example shows a daily intake goal of 1,470 calories and an over consumption of 1,396 calories. You actually could run that off in about 50 minutes—if you did six-minute miles. Eighty-five minutes on an elliptical trainer would do the trick as well. You may look at this and think it's a bit extreme, but it really isn't. Track your diet for a week and marvel at the results. All of this data was acquired through a user-friendly web page called myfitnesspal.com. You need to pull it up and use it every day. It also has a mobile app that can be used on your smart phone, and all you need to do is scan the bar code of whatever you're eating or drinking. If it doesn't have a bar code, start typing it in. Virtually every major restaurant is listed as well as thousands of foods. If you like to cook, just go to the recipe tab and key in the ingredients and number of servings, and it does the rest. There's an exercise tab that lets you track your workouts and simultaneously deducts the caloric burn from you daily calorie consumption.

Breakfast

	Calories	Carbs	Fat	Protein	Sodium
Fruit - Banana, 1 piece (medium - 118g)	105	27	0	1	1
Quaker - Old Fashioned Quaker Oats, 1/2 cup dry	150	27	3	5	0
Add Food	255	54	3	6	1
Quick Tools					

Lunch

Applebee's - Cowboy Burger, 1 Burger	1,310	99	75	60	3,070
Drink - Coke, 300 ml	161	40	0	0	38
Add Food	1,471	139	76	60	3,108
Quick Tools					

Dinner

Papa Johns' Pizza - Pepperoni & Sausage Original Crust, 2 slice	760	76	36	28	1,960
Bud Lite Beer, 24 oz.	220	0	0	0	0
Add Food	980	76	36	28	1,960
Quick Tools					

Snacks

Ruffles Potato Chips, 1 oz. about 12 chips	160	15	10	2	160
Add Food	160	15	10	2	160
Quick Tools					
Totals	2,866	284	124	96	5,229
Your Daily Goal	1,470	184	49	74	2,300
Remaining	-1,396	-100	-75	-22	-2,929

Goals that get tracked get backed (by subconscious motivational forces). For even more assistance to do all the above, an increasingly popular tool is FitBit. The small device clips to a wrist band and tracks steps, distance, calories burned and active minutes. An LED shows your progress against your goal.

In addition to taking responsibility for your health, there is one other general *lesson* to heed which will help you get and keep your house in order, i.e., all areas of your life work well enough that there are no constraining factors thwarting your goal to be a Top Producer. Rather than try and coach you on each aspect of your life, I will give you an exercise, a practice to live by, which will serve you well. Embracing this one habit can accelerate reaching your goals in any and all areas of your life: Identify each and every toleration and takes steps to eliminate them all. A *toleration* is simply something you have been putting up with, big or small, which detracts from your focus, energy, and power. When you eliminate something you have been stepping over or around, you will stop wasting energy on that, and you will become more present.

Right now would be an excellent time to get out your pen or keyboard and make a list of fifty things you are tolerating, at work or outside work, from small annoyances to seemingly insurmountable challenges. An example of a minor toleration is when you automatically reach for your favorite dress shirt, but then remember it's missing a button, and you tell yourself you need to get that fixed, over and over, for weeks. Sew on a button, delegate it to someone else to do, or give the shirt to Goodwill.

An example of a larger toleration which may take a few steps to resolve is when a colleague habitually draws you in to time-wasting, negative energy, counterproductive conversations. First, it is important to recognize and admit how putting up with this must have some pay-off for you, even if it's not a healthy one. You get something out of allowing this to go on. Once you see that, you can then see the obvious expense of this, and that being free of this toleration far outweighs letting it continue. When handling a toleration involves re-educating another person (whom you've been allowing to drain you) be gracious, definitive and firm. It is possible, and smart, to remain respectful and kind and not abrupt or righteous.

Look over your list and choose a few easy things to handle, and get them resolved today, or this week. If it is a multi-step item, such as organizing your entire office and desk, just write down the next action to take to make progress towards eliminating what you've been putting up with, and take that one next action. You will be amazed at the extra energy, time and self-esteem that comes even before you finish half your list. Resolve to become toleration-free, and you will be able to focus on everything you need to achieve your Top Producer goals.

What I have found over the years is that individuals that deal in financial sales, as with many other sales professions, can have a hard time focusing and achieving new levels if personal issues are in the way. You can read this book, and follow many of the concepts, but what's it all worth if you don't reach your ultimate goal of happiness?

**Being healthy engenders better work habits,
gives you more energy,
and can boost your confidence.**

Chapter 10
PUTTING IT ALL TOGETHER

Now you have your corporate structure in place, your house is in order, and you have a few sales tips. How do you put everything that you have learned into practice? First and foremost, introductions are the key. Without them you have no pipeline, no presentations, and no sales. If you're on your own, you indeed have your work cut out for you; if you're in a bank setting, you may be somewhat ahead of the game. Either way, your first task is a little brainstorming.

While writing this book, my publisher gave me an exercise to complete that I like to refer to as "organized brainstorming." This was particularly useful because just arbitrarily writing things down on a piece of paper never accomplished much for me. My brain stormed, but that's about it. It is more productive to have a little direction in your endeavor. Your initial primary focus is introductions, so start writing down methods to increase your contact with people, and I would ask you to stretch that past the point of the obvious.

Earlier we touched on community activities, such as board affiliations and civic organizations. Jot down a few organizations that you feel may be beneficial as you seek introductions. They include your local business affiliations like the Chamber of Commerce, Downtown Alliance, and possibly a Rotary club. Then head into the nonprofit arena, perhaps the United Way, YMCA, or the Arts, if you prefer. Think of causes and areas that you feel strongly about, such as a shelter, soup kitchen, or church. All that you are looking for are ways to be introduced to other people and keep in mind, you must enjoy it. Don't volunteer for the Opera if you can't stand it—you won't get very far.

Now that you have a few of those written down, start listing people that you already know and think of how you can generate referrals. This is an easy assignment if you're in a bank. You will obviously write

77

down your branch managers, business bankers, private bankers, commercial lenders, and don't forget the executive officers. It's amazing how many times these close connections are never utilized.

You should also refer to every IRA you're assigned, because you have an embedded list of potential customers right at your fingertips. Nearly all of them have beneficiaries listed and very few financial professionals ever look at those as potential clients. Now I will say that this list can get a little tricky in south Florida, as many of the beneficiaries don't live here. However, if your practice is in a smaller or rural setting, they may live just down the street.

The next group is centers of influence, or COIs. This is usually comprised of lawyers, accountants, and many times people who are not initially top-of-mind. Realtors can be great COIs as they know when people are relocating to your community. I would recommend looking close to home as well. I've known advisors that have done well from home owners' associations, little league affiliations, church groups, and even parent-teacher organizations. The concept is to get involved with something that has the potential to create introductions.

What do I do now?

Probably the biggest pet peeve of mine is when I leave a seminar or some type of motivational meeting and I am excited and all set to move forward, to meet my goals, to implement what I've learned—but have no idea what to do first. That's what this chapter is intended to answer for you. As you go through this material and reflect on what you have read, we're going to put it all in a practical, usable format so that you can have the best day, week, month, and year of your career. And it all begins with a plan. I don't mean a sketchy document that you wrote on a napkin—an actual plan, with a format that you will learn to live by.

Goal-setting in a new way

You've probably heard countless times that you must write down your goals in order for them to be achieved. This is absolutely true; however, you must also include how you're going to achieve them. Then, taking actions one step at a time which are consistent with forwarding your goal, will lead you to what you want to achieve.

I begin with a very systematic plan for the week. I normally construct the plan for the next week on Friday afternoon. I'm generally in front of my calendar so I know what the week looks like. I also know what items could derail my week and I try to account for them. The worksheet enclosed on the following page is something that I developed and have found useful for a long time. If used methodically, any activity tracking method will improve results.

A few items to note:

- The entries must be proactive, meaning you don't get credit for "not" doing something. An example would be, "I'm not going to eat chicken wings." This would not go on the goal sheet. It may go on the penalty line, though, like on my chart (I like good wings).

- You have a maximum of 100 points for a given week and you CANNOT earn "extra credit" by doing more of something that you've planned; therefore there is no "make up" for penalty points.

- Don't self-destruct the plan. If you have plans for a Saturday fishing trip and you know your diet is getting blown, be realistic and plan around it. If you know that you're meeting friends for happy hour, don't penalize yourself for it, just plan for it.

Note that not everything on this list is business related; in fact just over half of my weekly points for this sample week are related to my profession. The list items are entirely up to you — just abide by the rules, see where it goes and you will be amazed at the results after just a few short weeks. This is an actual copy of one of my weekly sheets and was updated through Thursday of the week. I was rolling along at a pretty good pace, but you can see the impact of self-imposed penalties costing me 17 points for my Tuesday afternoon happy-hour. I don't recall the event, but it probably had something to do with a spring training baseball game.

The concept is to plan for *proactive* activities. Those are the important ones that get you where you want to go. *Reactive* activities are rarely good and can't be planned, hence the term, unless it's winning the lottery; but of course you had to buy the ticket so it's not entirely reactive.

I generally start the plan on a Monday as it works into my schedule far better than any other day of the week. I complete my list either Friday afternoon or over the preceding weekend, as my schedule is relatively accurate at that point. The goal-setting exercise is actually quite fulfilling as you prioritize all of those items that you want to accomplish.

At first it may seem slightly tedious, but as you reap the rewards, you will find it more fun and actually look forward to it. For all you perfectionists out there, a weekly score of 100 (although perfect) may indicate that you're not pushing yourself hard enough. This system should be used to challenge yourself and so some of the activities should be a stretch. If you already take fitness classes in the evenings, then a goal of going to the gym three times a week isn't really a meaningful goal. The list should be comprised of things that you want to accomplish and will be very proud of when you succeed.

A downloadable document is available on my web site, www.LessonsofaTopProducer.com and can be printed out and kept in a binder, or kept in an Excel file and updated on your computer. In the fall of 2014, this will be available in program format along with a mobile app so you can update it anytime.

Almost no goal is absurd or impossible to achieve if you have the right tools, system and coaching.

Chapter 11
WELCOME TO APOLLO SALES TRAINING
and **Jenny**™, the CRM with the "Human Element"

This chapter is a sales pitch. I'm a sales guy, and this is my pitch. I am not interested in you reading the book up to this point and then nothing changing. What I want to persuade you to do is utilize these lessons and actually achieve all of your Top Producer goals.

The Apollo Sales Training is a comprehensive two-year program designed specifically to utilize the practices of this book. It garners its name from the Apollo space travel missions of NASA that ran from 1961 to 1972, the program responsible for the first humans to land on the moon when Neil Armstrong and Buzz Aldrin first set foot on its surface July 20, 1969. This is not meant to compare the writings of this book and training program to the achievements of walking on the moon. It's intended to relay a mindset of "anything is possible" given the right environment, planning, and execution. The human race is defined by curiosity, exploration, and a constant, all-encompassing desire to improve. We are driven to competition, not just with our peers, but more importantly, with ourselves; we always strive to improve upon our past efforts. NASA's Apollo program is the perfect example of what our human ambitions, if nurtured, can produce.

Now, I am aware that there were probably ulterior motives during the time of the space race, but when someone sees a mountain and says "I'll climb it," or a race and says "I'm faster," or a rock in space and says, "I can get there," it is the paradigm of human existence.

In 1954 an English runner named Roger Bannister broke the acclaimed four-minute mile with a finishing time of 3:59.4. Two months later, Bannister and an Australian named John Landy both turned in finishing times of under four minutes with Landy losing at the finish line. Today, the four-minute mile is the standard among midrange male athletes. This is just another example of humans achieving things originally thought to be impossible.

If you've ever spent some time goal-setting, and later looked at what you wrote down and felt it was unrealistic, impossible, or absurd, it probably means you simply did not have the system, tools, and coaching you needed to achieve what your mind could conceive. What is being provided here can help you turn the "unrealistic" into "accomplished!"

The Apollo Sales Training is designed to guide and coach you through the steps of this book. It begins with a two-and-a-half-day session held in Sarasota, Florida. You and your classmates will begin a two-year journey as a unique cohort, beginning and finishing your program together and supporting each other along the way. You will continue the journey through six more two-and-a-half-day symposiums held every three months throughout the next two years, concluding with a graduation ceremony at the 24th month. As I mentioned earlier, planning, execution, and accountability are the keys to success in our business. This two-year program will offer you just that, as the symposiums are designed as planning exercises, building on the previous sessions and tracking ongoing results and accountability.

During the first session, you will be introduced to *Jenny*, *the CRM with the "Human Element."* Jenny is a proprietary client relationship management (CRM) system that is available exclusively to class participants and graduates of Apollo Sales Training. It is monitored by a staff of full-time sales assistants dedicated to helping you succeed. Preloaded with all of your client's non-sensitive information, Jenny is voice-activated.

Picture yourself after your fist successful client event: you have done everything by the book and it worked to perfection. You've spoken to countless people, made some great introductions, and even booked a couple of appointments. Now the party is over and you're trying to recall the many conversations that you had, with whom and about what.

You know it would be better to write those notes out right then instead of trying to keep it all straight in your head until you go into the office the next day. But, that feels like work and you are ready to finally end your work day. But what if it were as easy as telling a friend? Picture tapping a few buttons on your smartphone, speaking the new contact's name, and giving a brief description of your conversation. Now I know that this can be done with a recording device, however, the following day your recording device can't load the new contact data into your database and automatically categorize it as an "introduction" with your notes transcribed, ready for review. As soon as you log on to the system, you'll be greeted with a pop-up screen saying, "Good morning Don, it looks like you had a great event last night. Shall I start the follow-up procedures?" Welcome to the human element.

Weekly Activity Chart

	Goal	Mon	Tue	Wed	Thu	Fri	Sat	Sun	Actual	Notes
Activity										
Professional										
5 new introductions (2 pts ea)	10		4	2					6	
Attend 2 community events (2 pts ea)	4		2	2					4	
Write 5,000 words for the next book	10				10				10	
Credit request XXXX	10		10						10	
Follow up with XYZ Company	5				5				5	
Follow up with Tiger Woods	10		10						10	
RFP for quarterly meeting	5		5						5	
Physical										
MyFitnesspal.com daily update	7	1	1	1	1				4	
Under calorie count (1 pt per day)	6	1		1	1				3	Saturday BBQ/ Off day
One hour workout (1 pt ea/ max 6)	6	1	1	1	1				4	
Eat a salad for lunch (1 pt ea/ 4 max)	4		1	1	1				3	
Up by 5:30 (1 pt ea/ off Sat)	6	1	1		1				3	Over slept Wednesday
Mental										
Read Lessons of a Top Producer	10			10					10	Finished book Wed
Emotional										
Send you wife flowers	2				2				2	
Spiritual										
Bible Study on Wednesday	5			5					5	
Total Points	100	4	35	23	22	0	0	0	84	
Penalties										
More than 2 alcoholic beverages/ day			2						2	2 points per day/ 3 Tue
More than 6 alcoholic beverages/ week										10 point penalty
Smoking (at all)										15 point penalty
Happy Hour (Non required)			15						15	10 point penalty
Chicken wings										5 point penalty
Total Penalties	17		17						17	
Net Score	83	4	18	23	22				67	

If you're in front of your desk, you can key in any instructions you'd like for follow-up, or if you happen to be on the road, a few buttons on the smart phone and some instructions will work just fine. You probably have a pocket full of business cards from the evening's event that you could key into the system, or just scan them, or maybe just take a picture of them with your smartphone. Within a short time, all information will be entered, awaiting your instructions. If a few days go by with no instructions, Jenny will kindly remind you that you have introductions awaiting your follow-up. "She" does not do this through a boilerplate email, but as a person on the other side of a pop-up window asking if there's anything needed to assist you.

Even though the voice transcription service is automated, it is monitored by your dedicated sales assistants, edited for typos, and entered into the client database ready for your review and approval before submission to the client's permanent record. Once approved, notes can be kept as *private* (meaning only you can see them) or *public* (meaning anyone authorized can view the data, including your compliance department). Public notes remain on file indefinitely and can be used in legal proceedings; private notes are precisely that—they can be viewed only by you and your delegates and may be deleted any time.

Since the transcription is monitored by a real human, don't limit the instructions to just client updates and notes—Jenny will also take instructions. Need to schedule a follow-up call to a certain client on a certain day at a certain time? A moment on your smartphone is all it takes, just like leaving a voicemail message. Jenny can also execute certain client-related tasks, although they must be pre-approved through your compliance department. She can't call a client to let them know a bond matured; she can, however, send out your pre-appointment packets, holiday and birthday cards, appointment reminders, and flowers to your wife. Keep in mind that Jenny is not politically correct and has no real office etiquette so she does need a little supervision. Her job is to make you better at yours, and if that involves making reservations for your 15th anniversary dinner, it's all good with her. If some help is needed to plan and coordinate a client event, no problem at all—just let Jenny know what you want.

Jenny is wonderful when it comes to client interactions as well. If you're meeting at your office, she's right there with you(in the upper right corner of your screen), or if you prefer, you may pull up the client information and enter data yourself. If you're traveling between appointments, go back to the smartphone again for a quick voice transmission file relating to your last appointment. But what if this was the first appointment and there's no client information on the system? It's quite okay with Jenny, as the next time you log on, that friendly little pop-up box that you're really beginning to love will say,

"Good morning Don, looks like you had a great appointment yesterday. Can I get some more information about [the new name] and do we need to do any follow up?"

A few other interesting capabilities of *Jenny*™':

- Tracks expenses and assigns them to client files with just a picture of a receipt.

- Tracks revenue on a client level for revenue/ cost analysis.

- Provides proposal illustrations for every carrier your firm has approved.

- Handles financial statement input to any financial and investment planning software.

- Produces compliance-approved correspondence.

- Allows you unlimited notes, both public and private.

- Helps you with almost anything else that you can think of!

Now that we know about Jenny and what she can do, we'll move into the organized brainstorming session. This is an exercise we spoke of in earlier chapters, but as a tool it works much better in a group environment. You and your classmates will come up with countless ideas of how to find more introductions, organize the data, and form an action plan to be implemented upon your return to the field. We will also delve into your existing book of business, how to attract referrals, and improve your database by asking questions about contacts' other advisors, such as attorneys and CPAs. The goal of this session is to provide you with tools to significantly increase the quantity of introductions over the next three months.

You will also be introduced to a scoring system which is a method used to track results. Since many of your classmates may not be judged on revenue alone, I use a scoring system to track results on a quarterly basis. Your first day of class, you have a rating of "100" and the scoring system is comprised of revenue, possibly number of clients, deposit and loan balances, and even personal data which you may have included in your Weekly Activity Goals. In fact, your Activity Chart weekly score is included in your rating, so make sure it's updated every week. At the end of the three months, you will be given a confidential rating of your progress. All data is compiled for the class using the ratings without name identification and aggregated so the class may benefit from results, without reprisals for underperforming classmates. Keep in mind the intent is not to humiliate, but rather to improve. I'm certain that all of you competitive-minded individuals out there will form some sort of pool based on rating scores. You will be able to see the results first hand as you continue through the program—and your paycheck may also be improving along the way!

During the next two years, you and your colleagues will meet about every 12 weeks, during which time we will review the results since the last meeting, develop corrective actions, and make new plans to achieve goals before the next scheduled symposium. This is what I call forced accountability. It also provides you with a powerful support group that will last long past graduation day.

Your training will conclude approximately 24 months from the starting point with a celebration of a successful journey. By now you know the principles of this material, and how to implement and account for them—you've been consistently doing it for two years. Don't worry though, the ongoing support will continue and that little pop-up window that you've come to adore will still be there telling you "good morning" and asking if they can assist you with your busy schedule of the day.

With all that you have learned over the time of this class, hopefully you will realize that anything is possible if planned accordingly, implemented according to plan, and you're held accountable for results (Rome wasn't built in a day, but it was built!).

I am constantly amazed at the power of human ingenuity and the passion for excellence. We see it every day and probably don't even notice. We have all chosen a wonderful profession. You are entrusted with something that for most people ranks near the top of their "things most important in my life" list, usually just under "health" and "family." With this responsibility entrusted to us as advisors, we must do our jobs effectively, going above all of the expectations of both clients and employers; and we must practice the utmost of integrity as this responsibility should never be taken for granted.

"The ones who are crazy enough to think that they can change the world are the ones who do."

—*Steve Jobs*

ACKNOWLEDGEMENTS

This book is a culmination of my experiences derived from other top producers, iconic sales managers and program directors, clients, and dear friends. Thank you to all of the readers of my many business plans that have read more like dissertations, and their urging to write a book. I would like to thank all that have contributed to this writing with special thanks to David Biliter, Executive Vice President and Director of Sales at Arvest Asset Management, and my former sales manager and mentor. David taught me not only how to manage an investment program, but how to manage people. He has impeccable integrity, and has been in true inspiration to me over the past 11 years.

Also special thanks to Jim Nonnengard, President of Regions Investment Services. Although my tenure with Jim was a brief one due to bank mergers, he never allowed anyone to believe that they couldn't accomplish greatness. Under his leadership I earned the highest accolades given by our employer. Even though the bar seemed unreachable at the time, he not only expected me to reach it, he somehow just knew that I would.

Thank you to my book reviewers, Geoff Shea, Wayne Scott, and Steve Altier, all of whom I have known and respected for many years; your public review of this writing is greatly appreciated.

Thank you to my publisher, Suncoast Digital Press, and its wonderful staff of professionals, particularly Barbara Bingham, for spending countless hours editing my work, many times in the wee hours of the morning, and for convincing me that I could indeed write and publish a book.

With much gratitude, I acknowledge my wife Jennifer, who has endured the effects of the great recession first hand. Her steadfast approach to raising our family through good economic times and bad ones has been an inspiration to this writing. My hope is that it lives up to her expectations.

I want to acknowledge my father, Rev. Donald Watson, Sr., a man that dedicated his entire life to helping others not only through spirituality, but through a genuine caring for one's overall wellbeing. What he did not pass on in business and financial acumen, he did in an unwavering sense of integrity and spirituality, as he preached every Sunday morning that we will all eventually be answering to a higher authority. This message has influenced every aspect of my business career over the years. Whether managing clients' assets, employees' careers, or our daily lives, it must be done with integrity and honesty in order to be fulfilled.

While *Lessons of a Top Producer* is full of actionable recommendations and practical steps, the character and values I've learned from far too many people to mention by name, but must thank nonetheless, must not be overlooked.

---- Don Watson

Download your FREE REPORT by Top Producer Don Watson by visiting www.LessonsofaTopProducer.com. In this report you will learn the secrets to having a "seamless strategy" which places you in the path of opportunities, no matter where you are, without ever compromising yourself or your reputation.

When you visit the web site, you'll find complete information about The Apollo Sales Training and a calendar of upcoming events and training classes. Check and see if Don Watson is already scheduled to speak in your city, or make your request to engage him.

The web site is also where you can find information on **quantity book orders** for your company and sales force.

Lessons of a Top Producer, ©2014,
is available in paperback and eBook formats on Amazon.com.

Suncoast Digital Press, Inc. is a publishing company in Sarasota, Florida. For more information on this author or other books published by Suncoast Digital Press, Inc., visit www.SuncoastDigitalPress.com.

35414304R00064

Made in the USA
Lexington, KY
10 September 2014